OPERATING SYSTEMS 101

NOVICE TO EXPERT

WINDOWS, LINUX, UNIX, IOS AND ANDROID

5 BOOKS IN 1

BOOK 1
WINDOWS MASTERY: A BEGINNER'S GUIDE TO OPERATING SYSTEMS

BOOK 2
LINUX UNLEASHED: FROM NOVICE TO SYSTEM ADMINISTRATOR

BOOK 3
UNLOCKING UNIX: ADVANCED TECHNIQUES FOR OPERATING SYSTEM VETERANS

BOOK 4
IOS DEMYSTIFIED: EXPERT INSIGHTS INTO APPLE'S OPERATING SYSTEM

BOOK 5
ANDROID ENGINEERING: MASTERING THE WORLD'S MOST POPULAR MOBILE OS

ROB BOTWRIGHT

Published by Rob Botwright
Library of Congress Cataloging-in-Publication Data
ISBN 978-1-83938-719-7
Cover design by Rizzo

Disclaimer

The contents of this book are based on extensive research and the best available historical sources. However, the author and publisher make no claims, promises, or guarantees about the accuracy, completeness, or adequacy of the information contained herein. The information in this book is provided on an "as is" basis, and the author and publisher disclaim any and all liability for any errors, omissions, or inaccuracies in the information or for any actions taken in reliance on such information. The opinions and views expressed in this book are those of the author and do not necessarily reflect the official policy or position of any organization or individual mentioned in this book. Any reference to specific people, places, or events is intended only to provide historical context and is not intended to defame or malign any group, individual, or entity. The information in this book is intended for educational and entertainment purposes only. It is not intended to be a substitute for professional advice or judgment. Readers are encouraged to conduct their own research and to seek professional advice where appropriate. Every effort has been made to obtain necessary permissions and acknowledgments for all images and other copyrighted material used in this book. Any errors or omissions in this regard are unintentional, and the author and publisher will correct them in future editions.

BOOK 1 - WINDOWS MASTERY: A BEGINNER'S GUIDE TO OPERATING SYSTEMS

BOOK 2 - LINUX UNLEASHED: FROM NOVICE TO SYSTEM ADMINISTRATOR

BOOK 3 - UNLOCKING UNIX: ADVANCED TECHNIQUES FOR OPERATING SYSTEM VETERANS

BOOK 4 - IOS DEMYSTIFIED: EXPERT INSIGHTS INTO APPLE'S OPERATING SYSTEM

BOOK 5 - ANDROID ENGINEERING: MASTERING THE WORLD'S MOST POPULAR MOBILE OS

Introduction

Welcome to "Operating Systems 101: Novice to Expert," a comprehensive book bundle designed to take you on a journey through the fascinating world of operating systems. In this bundle, we explore five of the most prominent operating systems, covering Windows, Linux, UNIX, iOS, and Android, catering to readers at all levels of expertise.

Book 1, "Windows Mastery: A Beginner's Guide to Operating Systems," serves as an entry point for those new to operating systems, providing a solid foundation in the fundamentals of Windows.

Book 2, "Linux Unleashed: From Novice to System Administrator," takes readers on a deep dive into the Linux operating system, equipping them with the knowledge and skills needed to become proficient Linux users and system administrators.

Book 3, "Unlocking UNIX: Advanced Techniques for Operating System Veterans," explores the advanced features and techniques of UNIX, offering insights into its powerful capabilities for seasoned operating system veterans.

Book 4, "iOS Demystified: Expert Insights into Apple's Operating System," provides an in-depth exploration of iOS, Apple's renowned operating system for mobile devices, offering expert-level insights into its architecture, features, and development.

Book 5, "Android Engineering: Mastering the World's Most Popular Mobile OS," delves into the intricacies of the Android operating system, empowering readers to become proficient in developing and managing applications for the Android platform.

Whether you are a beginner looking to build a strong foundation or an expert seeking to deepen your understanding, "Operating Systems 101: Novice to Expert" has something for everyone. Join us on this enlightening journey as we unlock the mysteries of operating systems and empower you to become a proficient user, developer, or administrator across a diverse range of platforms.

BOOK 1

WINDOWS MASTERY

A BEGINNER'S GUIDE TO OPERATING SYSTEMS

ROB BOTWRIGHT

Chapter 1: Introduction to Windows: Navigating the Interface

Windows Start Menu and Taskbar play a pivotal role in the user experience of Microsoft Windows operating systems, offering convenient access to applications, settings, and system utilities. The Start Menu, initially introduced in Windows 95, underwent significant changes over the years, evolving to meet users' needs and preferences. In Windows 10 and beyond, the Start Menu blends the familiarity of traditional menu-based navigation with modern features like Live Tiles, enabling users to customize their desktop experience.

Navigating the Start Menu is intuitive; users can simply click on the Start button or press the Windows key on their keyboard to open it. From there, they can access a variety of items, including recently used applications, pinned applications, and system folders. Additionally, the Start Menu provides a search bar, allowing users to quickly find and launch programs or files by typing keywords.

Customizing the Start Menu is straightforward and can be tailored to suit individual preferences.

Users can resize the Start Menu by dragging its edges, rearrange or resize Live Tiles, and pin or unpin applications for easy access. Moreover, the "Settings" app offers extensive customization options, allowing users to personalize the Start Menu layout, choose which folders appear, and toggle various settings such as showing recently added apps or suggestions.

The Taskbar, located at the bottom of the screen by default, serves as a multi-functional tool for managing open windows, accessing frequently used applications, and monitoring system status. It provides quick access to running programs through pinned icons, system notifications, and the system tray. Users can also customize the Taskbar by pinning their favorite apps, rearranging icons, and adjusting settings such as hiding or showing labels and taskbar location.

To pin an application to the Taskbar, users can simply right-click on its icon in the Start Menu or desktop and select "Pin to taskbar." Alternatively, they can drag and drop the application's icon directly onto the Taskbar. This allows for easy access to frequently used programs, eliminating the need to navigate through the Start Menu each time.

Furthermore, the Taskbar hosts several system icons and indicators, including the clock, volume control, network status, and notifications. Users can interact with these icons to adjust settings or view relevant information. For example, clicking on the network icon allows users to connect to available Wi-Fi networks or troubleshoot network issues.

In addition to its primary functions, the Taskbar supports various productivity-enhancing features and shortcuts. For instance, users can switch between open windows by clicking on their corresponding Taskbar icons or using keyboard shortcuts like Alt + Tab. Moreover, hovering the mouse cursor over a Taskbar icon displays thumbnail previews of open windows, facilitating quick window management and navigation.

For power users and productivity enthusiasts, mastering the Windows Start Menu and Taskbar can significantly improve efficiency and streamline workflow. By leveraging customization options, keyboard shortcuts, and productivity features, users can optimize their desktop experience and make the most out of their Windows operating system. Whether it's launching applications, managing open windows, or accessing system utilities, the Start Menu and Taskbar remain indispensable tools for Windows users worldwide.

File Explorer, a fundamental tool in the Windows

operating system, provides users with a graphical interface for navigating and managing files and folders stored on their computer. Accessed through the Start Menu or by pressing the Windows key + E shortcut, File Explorer offers a user-friendly environment for performing various file management tasks efficiently. Upon opening File Explorer, users are presented with a familiar interface consisting of a navigation pane on the left, a main window displaying file and folder contents, and a ribbon toolbar offering access to common file management actions.

Navigating through folders in File Explorer is intuitive; users can simply click on a folder to open it and view its contents. To move up one level in the folder hierarchy, users can click on the "Up" arrow button in the toolbar or use the keyboard shortcut Alt + Up arrow. Moreover, users can quickly navigate to frequently accessed folders by adding them to the Quick Access section in the navigation pane, eliminating the need to navigate through multiple levels of folders.

File Explorer offers various options for organizing and viewing files and folders. Users can sort files by name, date modified, size, or type by clicking on the corresponding column header in the main window. Additionally, users can change the view mode to suit their preferences, choosing between

Extra Large Icons, Large Icons, Medium Icons, Small Icons, List, Details, Tiles, and Content views. To change the view mode, users can click on the "View" tab in the ribbon toolbar and select their desired view mode from the "Layout" group.

File Explorer also provides powerful search capabilities, allowing users to quickly locate files and folders by entering keywords or search criteria in the search box located at the top-right corner of the window. Users can refine their search results by specifying search filters such as file type, date modified, or size. Alternatively, users can use advanced search operators such as AND, OR, NOT, and quotation marks to perform complex searches.

In addition to basic file management tasks, File Explorer enables users to perform a wide range of file operations, including copying, moving, renaming, deleting, and compressing files and folders. To copy or move files, users can simply drag and drop them from one location to another within File Explorer or between File Explorer windows. Alternatively, users can use the keyboard shortcuts Ctrl + C to copy and Ctrl + V to paste files. Similarly, to rename a file or folder, users can right-click on it, select "Rename," and enter the new name.

File Explorer also supports batch file operations, allowing users to perform actions on multiple files or folders simultaneously. To select multiple files or folders, users can hold down the Ctrl key while clicking on each item or use the Shift key to select a range of items. Once selected, users can perform various file operations on the selected items, such as copying, moving, deleting, or compressing them.

Furthermore, File Explorer integrates seamlessly with other Windows features and applications, enabling users to perform tasks such as sharing files via email, printing documents, and burning files to optical discs directly from the File Explorer interface. Users can access these features by right-clicking on a file or folder and selecting the desired action from the context menu.

For advanced users and power users, File Explorer offers additional features and customization options to enhance productivity and efficiency. Users can customize the Quick Access section, customize the ribbon toolbar, configure folder options and view settings, and create custom libraries to organize files across multiple locations. Moreover, users can create shortcuts to frequently used folders or network locations and pin them to the Quick Access section for easy access.

In summary, File Explorer serves as a versatile and indispensable tool for managing files and folders in the Windows operating system. Whether performing basic file operations, organizing files, or searching for specific items, File Explorer offers a robust set of features and intuitive interface designed to meet the needs of users at all levels of expertise. By mastering File Explorer basics and exploring its advanced features, users can streamline their file management workflow and maximize productivity in their daily computing tasks.

Chapter 2: Getting Started with File Management

Creating and managing folders is a fundamental aspect of file organization in any operating system, including Windows. In Windows, users can easily create new folders to organize their files and documents in a structured manner, facilitating efficient retrieval and management. One of the simplest methods to create a new folder is by using the graphical user interface provided by File Explorer. To create a new folder using File Explorer, users can navigate to the location where they want to create the folder, right-click on an empty space within the window, and select "New" from the context menu. From the submenu that appears, users can then choose "Folder," which will create a new folder with the default name "New Folder." Alternatively, users can press the Ctrl + Shift + N keys simultaneously to create a new folder directly. Once the new folder is created, users can rename it by right-clicking on it, selecting "Rename" from the context menu, and entering the desired name. Moreover, users can also create nested folders by repeating the same process within an existing folder, allowing for hierarchical organization of files and subfolders.

While creating folders via the graphical interface is convenient for most users, advanced users and power users may prefer to use the command-line interface (CLI) for greater efficiency and automation. In Windows, the Command Prompt or PowerShell provides a powerful environment for executing various commands and scripts, including those related to file and folder management. To create a new folder using the Command Prompt, users can open the Command Prompt window and navigate to the desired location using the "cd" command. Once in the desired directory, users can use the "mkdir" command followed by the name of the new folder to create it. For example, to create a new folder named "Documents" in the current directory, users can type "mkdir Documents" and press Enter. Similarly, in PowerShell, users can use the "New-Item" cmdlet with the "-ItemType" parameter set to "Directory" to create a new folder. For instance, users can type "New-Item -ItemType Directory -Name Documents" and press Enter to create a new folder named "Documents" in the current directory. Additionally, users can specify the full path of the folder to create it in a specific location.

Once folders are created, users can manage them effectively to maintain a well-organized file system. File Explorer provides various options for managing folders, including renaming, moving, copying, and deleting folders. To rename a folder in File Explorer, users can right-click on the folder, select "Rename" from the context menu, and enter the new name. Alternatively, users can select the folder and press the F2 key to initiate the renaming process. To move or copy a folder to a different location, users can drag and drop the folder to the desired destination within File Explorer. Additionally, users can use the "Cut" and "Paste" commands from the context menu or keyboard shortcuts (Ctrl + X for cut, Ctrl + V for paste) to move or copy folders. Similarly, users can delete folders by selecting them and pressing the Delete key or using the "Delete" command from the context menu. Alternatively, users can use the "rmdir" command in the Command Prompt or the "Remove-Item" cmdlet in PowerShell to delete folders from the command line.

In addition to basic folder management tasks, users can also customize folder properties and settings to suit their preferences. In File Explorer, users can right-click on a folder and select "Properties" from the context menu to access the folder's properties dialog box. From there, users can customize various properties such as the folder's name, location, attributes, and permissions. For example, users can set the folder to be hidden or read-only, specify custom icons or labels, and configure sharing and security settings. Moreover, users can create shortcuts to folders for quick access or customize folder views and sorting options within File Explorer to optimize file organization and navigation.

Overall, creating and managing folders is a fundamental skill that every Windows user should master to maintain an organized and efficient file system. Whether using the graphical interface provided by File Explorer or the command-line interface of the Command Prompt or PowerShell, users can create, rename, move, copy, and delete folders with ease. By adopting best practices for folder organization and management, users can enhance productivity, streamline workflow, and ensure that their files and documents are easily accessible when needed.

Copying, moving, and deleting files are essential tasks in file management, allowing users to organize and manage their data efficiently. In Windows, these operations can be performed using both the graphical user interface (GUI) provided by File Explorer and the command-line interface (CLI) offered by Command Prompt or PowerShell. File Explorer offers an intuitive interface for performing these tasks, making it accessible to users of all levels of expertise. To copy a file using File Explorer, users can navigate to the file they want to copy, right-click on it, and select "Copy" from the context menu. Alternatively, users can select the file and use the keyboard shortcut Ctrl + C to copy it. Once the file is copied, users can navigate to the destination folder, right-click on an empty space within the folder, and select "Paste" from the context menu. This will create a copy of the file in the destination folder, preserving the original file in its original location. Similarly, users can move a file by selecting it, dragging it to the desired destination folder within File Explorer, and releasing the mouse button. Alternatively, users can use the keyboard shortcuts Ctrl + X to cut the file and Ctrl + V to paste it into the destination folder, effectively moving the file. Furthermore, File Explorer offers options for deleting files, allowing users to remove unwanted or unnecessary files from their system. To delete a file, users can select it and press the Delete key on their keyboard or right-click on the file and select "Delete" from the context menu. Users can also use the keyboard shortcut Shift + Delete to permanently delete a file without sending it to the Recycle Bin. Additionally, File Explorer provides options for restoring deleted files from the Recycle Bin or permanently deleting them from the system. While File Explorer offers a user-friendly interface for copying, moving, and deleting files, advanced users and power users may prefer to use the command-line interface (CLI) for greater efficiency and automation. In Windows, the Command Prompt and PowerShell provide powerful environments for executing various commands and scripts related to file and folder management. To copy a file using the Command Prompt, users can open the Command Prompt window, navigate to the directory containing the file they want to copy using the "cd" command, and use the "copy" command followed by the filename and destination directory. For example, to copy a file named "example.txt" from the current directory to a directory named "backup," users can type "copy example.txt backup" and press Enter. Similarly, in PowerShell, users can use the "Copy-Item" cmdlet to copy files. For example, users can type "Copy-Item example.txt backup" and press Enter to copy the file "example.txt" to the "backup" directory. To move a file using the Command Prompt, users can use the "move" command followed by the filename and destination directory. For example, to move a file named "example.txt" from the current directory to a directory named "archive," users can type "move example.txt archive" and press Enter. Similarly, in PowerShell, users can use the "Move-Item" cmdlet to move files. For example, users can type "Move-Item example.txt archive" and press Enter to move the file "example.txt" to the "archive" directory. Furthermore, users can delete files using the command-line interface. In the Command Prompt, users can use the "del" command followed by the filename to delete a file. For example, to delete a file named "example.txt," users can type "del example.txt" and press Enter. Additionally, users can use the "rd" command followed by the directory name to delete a directory and all its contents. In PowerShell, users can use the "Remove-Item" cmdlet to delete files and directories. For example, to delete a file named "example.txt," users can type "Remove-Item example.txt" and press Enter. Similarly, to delete a directory and all its contents, users can use the "Remove-Item" cmdlet with the "-Recurse" parameter. For example, to delete a directory named "backup" and all its contents, users can type "Remove-Item backup -Recurse" and press

Enter. In summary, copying, moving, and deleting files are essential tasks in file management, allowing users to organize and manage their data effectively. Whether using the graphical user interface provided by File Explorer or the command-line interface offered by Command Prompt or PowerShell, users can perform these operations with ease and efficiency. By mastering these techniques, users can maintain a well-organized file system and streamline their workflow in Windows.

Chapter 3: Customizing Your Desktop Environment

Personalizing the desktop background and themes is an integral aspect of customizing the visual appearance of a computer's user interface, allowing users to tailor their computing environment to reflect their preferences and personality. In Windows operating systems, such as Windows 10, users have the flexibility to choose from a variety of desktop backgrounds, colors, and themes to create a personalized and visually appealing desktop experience. One of the simplest ways to personalize the desktop background in Windows is by right-clicking on an empty space on the desktop, selecting "Personalize" from the context menu, and navigating to the "Background" settings. From there, users can choose from a selection of pre-installed background images or browse their computer for a custom image to set as the desktop background. Additionally, users can customize the background settings further by selecting the desired picture position, such as "Fill," "Fit," "Stretch," "Tile," or "Center," to adjust how the image is displayed on the desktop.

Moreover, users can also set a slideshow of multiple images as the desktop background, with options to customize the slideshow duration and choose specific folders for the images. Furthermore, Windows provides options to personalize the desktop themes, which include settings for desktop background, colors, sounds, and mouse cursor. To access the desktop themes settings, users can again right-click on an empty space on the desktop, select "Personalize," and navigate to the "Themes" settings. From there, users can choose from a selection of pre-installed themes or create their own custom themes by mixing and matching background images, colors, and sounds. Additionally, users can further customize the themes by adjusting individual settings, such as accent color, sound scheme, and mouse cursor style. Moreover, Windows offers the option to download and install additional themes from the Microsoft Store, providing users with a wide range of options to personalize their desktop experience. While personalizing the desktop background and themes through the graphical user interface is convenient for most users, advanced users and power users may prefer to use the command-line interface (CLI) for greater control and automation. In Windows, the Command Prompt and PowerShell provide powerful environments for executing various commands and scripts related to desktop customization. To change the desktop background using the Command Prompt, users can use the "reg" command to modify the Windows Registry settings. For example, to set a custom image as the desktop background, users can run the following command: reg add "HKEY_CURRENT_USER\Control Panel\Desktop" /v Wallpaper /t REG_SZ /d "C:\Path\To\Image.jpg" /f This command modifies the "Wallpaper" value in the Windows Registry to point to the specified image file. Similarly, users can use the "reg" command to change other desktop settings, such as the picture position and slideshow options. In PowerShell, users can use the "Set-ItemProperty" cmdlet to modify registry values. For example, to set a custom image as the desktop background, users can run the following command: Set-ItemProperty -Path "HKCU:\Control Panel\Desktop" -Name Wallpaper -Value "C:\Path\To\Image.jpg" This command achieves the same result as the previous command but using PowerShell syntax. Furthermore, users can automate desktop customization tasks using batch files or PowerShell scripts, allowing for bulk changes to desktop settings across multiple computers. In summary, personalizing the desktop

background and themes is an essential aspect of creating a personalized and visually appealing computing environment in Windows. Whether using the graphical user interface provided by Windows settings or the command-line interface offered by Command Prompt or PowerShell, users can customize their desktop experience to reflect their preferences and personality. By mastering these techniques, users can create a desktop environment that is both functional and aesthetically pleasing, enhancing their overall computing experience.
Customizing the taskbar and system tray is a crucial aspect of personalizing the user experience in Windows operating systems, offering users the flexibility to tailor their desktop environment to their preferences and workflow. In Windows 10, the taskbar serves as a central hub for accessing frequently used applications, managing open windows, and monitoring system status, while the system tray provides quick access to system notifications, settings, and background processes. One of the simplest ways to customize the taskbar in Windows 10 is by right-clicking on an empty space on the taskbar and selecting "Taskbar settings" from the context menu. This opens the taskbar settings window, where users can customize various aspects of the taskbar's

appearance and functionality. For example, users can choose to auto-hide the taskbar when not in use, change its location on the screen, resize it, or enable small taskbar buttons for a more compact layout. Additionally, users can customize which icons appear on the taskbar by toggling individual system icons on or off, such as the clock, volume control, network status, and action center. Furthermore, users can choose which apps are pinned to the taskbar for quick access by right-clicking on an app's icon in the taskbar and selecting "Pin to taskbar" from the context menu. Similarly, users can unpin apps from the taskbar by right-clicking on their icons and selecting "Unpin from taskbar." Moreover, Windows 10 allows users to customize the system tray icons and notifications to suit their preferences. To customize system tray icons, users can click on the "Select which icons appear on the taskbar" link in the taskbar settings window. This opens a list of system icons that users can toggle on or off to control which icons appear in the system tray. Additionally, users can customize the behavior of system tray notifications by clicking on the "Turn system icons on or off" link and adjusting the settings for individual icons. For example, users can choose whether to show or hide notifications for volume control, network, power, and other system icons. While customizing the taskbar and system tray through the graphical user interface is convenient for most users, advanced users and power users may prefer to use the command-line interface (CLI) for greater control and automation. In Windows, the Command Prompt and PowerShell provide powerful environments for executing various commands and scripts related to taskbar and system tray customization. To customize the taskbar using the Command Prompt, users can use the "reg" command to modify the Windows Registry settings. For example, to auto-hide the taskbar, users can run the following command: reg add "HKEY_CURRENT_USER\Software\Microsoft\Windows\CurrentVersion\Explorer\StuckRects3" /v Settings /t REG_BINARY /d 2800000000000000003e00000000000000000000000 010000000 /f This command modifies the "Settings" value in the Windows Registry to enable auto-hide for the taskbar. Similarly, users can use the "reg" command to customize other taskbar settings, such as taskbar location, size, and button size. In PowerShell, users can use the "Set-ItemProperty" cmdlet to modify registry values. For example, to change the taskbar location to the top of the screen, users can run the following command: Set-ItemProperty -Path

"HKCU:\Software\Microsoft\Windows\CurrentVersion\Explorer\Taskband" -Name "UseOLEDTaskbarTransparency" -Value 0 This command modifies the "UseOLEDTaskbarTransparency" value in the Windows Registry to disable transparency for the taskbar. Additionally, users can automate taskbar and system tray customization tasks using batch files or PowerShell scripts, allowing for bulk changes across multiple computers. In summary, customizing the taskbar and system tray is essential for creating a personalized and efficient desktop environment in Windows 10. Whether using the graphical user interface provided by Windows settings or the command-line interface offered by Command Prompt or PowerShell, users can tailor their taskbar and system tray to their preferences and workflow. By mastering these techniques, users can optimize their desktop experience and enhance productivity in their daily computing tasks.

Chapter 4: Understanding User Accounts and Security

User account types and permissions are critical components of system security and access control in any operating system, including Windows. In Windows, user accounts are classified into several types, each with its own set of privileges and restrictions, designed to ensure the security and integrity of the system. The most common types of user accounts in Windows are local accounts and domain accounts. Local accounts are created and managed locally on a single computer, while domain accounts are managed centrally by a network domain controller in an Active Directory domain environment. Additionally, Windows also supports special types of user accounts, such as built-in accounts and guest accounts, each serving specific purposes in system administration and user management.

Local user accounts are the most basic type of user accounts in Windows, providing individual users with access to a single computer. These accounts are typically used for personal or home use, allowing users to customize their desktop environment and install applications according to their preferences. Local user accounts can have different levels of access and permissions, depending on their assigned user group and security settings. For example, standard user accounts have limited privileges and cannot make system-wide changes or install software without administrator approval, while administrator accounts have full control over the system and can perform administrative tasks, such as installing software, modifying system settings, and managing other user accounts.

To create a local user account in Windows, users can use the graphical user interface provided by the Control Panel or the Settings app. In the Control Panel, users can navigate to "User Accounts" and select "Manage another account" to access the user account management options. From there, users can choose to create a new account and specify whether it should be a standard user account or an administrator account. Similarly, in the Settings app, users can navigate to "Accounts" and select "Family & other users" to add a new user account. Users can then follow the prompts to enter the user's name, password, and account type.

In addition to local user accounts, Windows also supports domain user accounts, which are used in networked environments managed by Active

Directory. Domain user accounts are created and managed centrally by a domain administrator and can be accessed from any computer joined to the domain. These accounts provide users with access to network resources, such as shared folders, printers, and applications, based on their assigned permissions and group memberships. Domain user accounts are often used in business and enterprise environments to facilitate centralized user management and access control across multiple computers and servers.

To create a domain user account in Windows, users must have administrative privileges on the domain controller or be delegated the necessary permissions by a domain administrator. Domain user accounts can be created using the Active Directory Users and Computers snap-in, which is accessible from the Administrative Tools menu on the domain controller. In the Active Directory Users and Computers snap-in, users can navigate to the appropriate organizational unit (OU) or container, right-click on it, and select "New" > "User" to create a new user account. Users can then follow the prompts to enter the user's name, username, password, and other account details.

In addition to standard user accounts, Windows also includes built-in user accounts that serve specific purposes in system administration and user management. These built-in accounts are created automatically during the installation of Windows and are used by the operating system and various system services to perform essential tasks. Examples of built-in accounts include the Administrator account, which has full control over the system and is used for system administration purposes, and the Guest account, which provides limited access to the system for temporary or guest users. Built-in accounts cannot be deleted or modified like standard user accounts, but their permissions and settings can be customized to suit specific requirements.

To manage built-in user accounts in Windows, users can use the graphical user interface provided by the Computer Management snap-in or the Command Prompt. In the Computer Management snap-in, users can navigate to "Local Users and Groups" and select "Users" to view a list of built-in user accounts. From there, users can right-click on a built-in user account and select "Properties" to modify its settings, such as password, group memberships, and account status. Similarly, users can use the "net user" command in the Command Prompt to manage built-in user accounts. For example, to reset the password for the Administrator account, users can run the following command: net user Administrator *

In summary, user account types and permissions are essential components of system security and access control in Windows. By understanding the different types of user accounts available in Windows and how to create, manage, and customize them, users can ensure the security and integrity of their system while providing individual users with the appropriate level of access and privileges. Whether using local user accounts for personal use or domain user accounts for business use, users can leverage the built-in tools and utilities provided by Windows to effectively manage user accounts and enforce access control policies across their environment.

Windows Security Essentials encompasses a range of tools and features designed to safeguard computers running the Windows operating system from various security threats, including viruses, malware, spyware, and other malicious software. As an integral component of Windows, Security Essentials provides users with essential security functionalities to protect their systems and data from cyber threats. One of the key features of Windows Security Essentials is Windows Defender Antivirus, a built-in antivirus program that helps detect and remove viruses, malware, and other malicious software from the system. Windows Defender Antivirus runs in the background, continuously scanning files, programs, and downloads for potential threats and alerting users if any suspicious activity is detected. Users can also perform manual scans of their system using Windows Defender Antivirus to ensure that their computer is free from malware and other security threats. To initiate a manual scan using Windows Defender Antivirus, users can open the Windows Security app, navigate to the "Virus & threat protection" section, and click on the "Scan options" button. From there, users can choose between quick, full, and custom scans, depending on their specific needs and preferences. Quick scans are faster but less thorough, focusing on areas of the system where malware is most likely to hide, such as the system memory and startup files. Full scans, on the other hand, are more comprehensive, scanning the entire system, including all files, folders, and drives, for any signs of malware or other security threats. Custom scans allow users to specify which files, folders, or drives they want to scan, providing greater flexibility and control over the scanning process. In addition to antivirus protection, Windows Security Essentials also includes other security features, such as Windows Firewall, which helps prevent unauthorized access to the system by blocking incoming and outgoing network traffic based on predefined rules and settings. Windows Firewall monitors network activity and automatically blocks any suspicious or potentially harmful connections, helping users keep their system safe from external threats, such as hackers and malware. Users can configure Windows Firewall settings to customize the level of protection and allow or block specific programs, ports, or protocols according to their preferences and security requirements. To configure Windows Firewall settings, users can open the Windows Security app, navigate to the "Firewall & network protection" section, and click on the "Advanced settings" link. From there, users can create inbound and outbound rules, specify allowed or blocked programs, and configure other firewall settings to enhance their system's security. Moreover, Windows Security Essentials includes other security tools and features, such as Windows Defender SmartScreen, which helps protect users from phishing attacks and malicious websites by warning them before they visit potentially harmful sites or download suspicious files. Windows Defender SmartScreen analyzes websites and files in real-time, using advanced algorithms and machine learning techniques to identify and block malicious content, such as phishing scams, malware, and other online threats. Users can enable or disable Windows Defender SmartScreen and customize its settings in the Windows Security app under the "App & browser control" section. Additionally, Windows Security Essentials includes Device Security, which helps protect users' devices and data by providing security recommendations and alerts about potential security issues or vulnerabilities. Device Security monitors the security status of the device, including antivirus protection, firewall settings, device encryption, and other security features, and alerts users if any security risks or vulnerabilities are detected. Users can review security recommendations and take appropriate action to address any security issues or improve their device's security posture. Overall, Windows Security Essentials offers a comprehensive suite of security tools and features to help users protect their computers and data from various security threats. By leveraging the built-in security functionalities provided by Windows Security Essentials, users can enhance their system's security and minimize the risk of malware infections, data breaches, and other cyber threats. Whether using Windows Defender Antivirus to scan for malware, configuring Windows Firewall to block unauthorized network traffic, or enabling Windows Defender SmartScreen to protect against phishing attacks, users can take proactive steps to safeguard their system and stay protected in an increasingly digital and connected world.

Chapter 5: Exploring Built-in Applications: From Calculator to Paint

Windows Calculator and Notepad are two essential utilities bundled with the Windows operating system, offering users versatile tools for mathematical calculations and text editing, respectively. Windows Calculator provides users with a wide range of mathematical functions and capabilities, making it suitable for both basic arithmetic tasks and complex scientific calculations. To access Windows Calculator, users can simply type "calculator" in the Windows search bar and press Enter, or navigate to "Start" > "Windows Accessories" > "Calculator" from the Start menu. Once opened, users are presented with a clean and intuitive interface that allows them to perform various mathematical operations, including addition, subtraction, multiplication, division, exponentiation, square roots, and trigonometric functions. Moreover, Windows Calculator offers different modes, such as Standard, Scientific, Programmer, and Date Calculation, each tailored to specific user needs and preferences. For example, the Scientific mode provides additional functions, such as logarithms, factorials, and exponential functions, while the Programmer mode offers tools for working with binary, octal, and hexadecimal numbers. Additionally, Windows Calculator includes a history feature that allows users to view and reuse previous calculations, as well as a built-in converter for converting between different units of measurement, such as length, weight, volume, and temperature. Furthermore, Windows Calculator supports keyboard shortcuts for efficient input and navigation, such as Ctrl + C to copy, Ctrl + V to paste, and Ctrl + H to switch between different modes. Overall, Windows Calculator is a versatile and user-friendly tool that caters to the mathematical needs of users across various disciplines and professions, from students and educators to engineers and scientists. Notepad, on the other hand, is a simple yet powerful text editor that provides users with a lightweight and efficient tool for creating and editing plain text documents. To access Notepad, users can type "notepad" in the Windows search bar and press Enter, or navigate to "Start" > "Windows Accessories" > "Notepad" from the Start menu. Once opened, users are presented with a minimalistic interface that allows them to quickly start typing and editing text without distractions. Notepad supports basic text editing features, such as cut, copy, paste, undo, and redo, as well as find and replace functionality for searching and replacing text within a document. Moreover, Notepad includes options for changing the font, font size, and word wrap settings, allowing users to customize their editing environment to suit their preferences. Additionally, Notepad supports opening and saving text files in various formats, including plain text (.txt), Unicode (.txt), and rich text format (.rtf), making it compatible with a wide range of applications and platforms. While Notepad lacks the advanced features and capabilities found in other text editors, such as Microsoft Word or Notepad++, its simplicity and ease of use make it an ideal choice for quickly jotting down notes, drafting simple documents, or editing configuration files and scripts. Furthermore, Notepad integrates seamlessly with other Windows applications and services, allowing users to open text files directly from File Explorer, attach them to emails, or copy and paste text between different applications. In addition to its primary use as a text editor, Notepad can also be used as a lightweight tool for writing and executing batch scripts and PowerShell scripts. For example, users can create a new text document in Notepad, write a series of command-line commands or PowerShell commands, save the document with a .bat or .ps1 file extension, and then execute the script from the command line or PowerShell console. This allows users to automate repetitive tasks, perform system maintenance, and customize their Windows environment to meet their specific needs and requirements. Overall, Windows Calculator and Notepad are two indispensable utilities that provide users with essential tools for mathematical calculations and text editing, respectively. Whether performing basic arithmetic operations, solving complex equations, drafting simple documents, or writing and executing scripts, these built-in Windows utilities offer users efficient and reliable solutions for a wide range of tasks and workflows. Paint and Snipping Tool are two essential applications included in the Windows operating system, providing users with versatile tools for creating, editing, and annotating images and screenshots. Paint, also known as Microsoft Paint, is a simple yet powerful graphics editor that has been a part of Windows for decades. It offers users a wide range of drawing and painting tools, making it suitable for both basic image editing tasks and more advanced graphic design projects. To access Paint, users can type "paint" in the Windows search bar and press Enter, or navigate to "Start"

> "Windows Accessories" > "Paint" from the Start menu. Once opened, users are presented with a blank canvas where they can start drawing, painting, or editing images. Paint includes various drawing tools, such as pencil, brush, eraser, and fill, as well as shapes, text, and a color picker for selecting and customizing colors. Additionally, Paint supports basic image editing features, such as cut, copy, paste, resize, rotate, and flip, allowing users to manipulate images with ease. Moreover, Paint includes options for adjusting brightness, contrast, and saturation, as well as applying effects, such as blur, sharpen, and emboss, to enhance or modify images. While Paint lacks the advanced features and capabilities found in professional graphic design software, such as Adobe Photoshop or GIMP, its simplicity and ease of use make it an ideal choice for quick image editing tasks, such as cropping photos, drawing diagrams, or adding annotations to screenshots.

Snipping Tool, on the other hand, is a screenshot utility that allows users to capture, annotate, and share screenshots of all or part of their screen. It provides users with flexible options for capturing screenshots, including full-screen, window, rectangular, and free-form snips, making it suitable for a wide range of screenshotting needs.

To access Snipping Tool, users can type "snipping tool" in the Windows search bar and press Enter, or navigate to "Start" > "Windows Accessories" > "Snipping Tool" from the Start menu. Once opened, users can choose the desired snipping mode from the drop-down menu and then click and drag the mouse cursor to select the area of the screen they want to capture. After capturing a screenshot, Snipping Tool displays the image in a new window where users can annotate it using various drawing tools, such as pen, highlighter, and eraser, as well as add text, shapes, and arrows to highlight important information. Moreover, Snipping Tool allows users to save the annotated screenshot as an image file, copy it to the clipboard, or share it directly via email or other applications. While Snipping Tool provides basic screenshotting and annotation capabilities, users looking for more advanced features may consider using Snip & Sketch, a newer and more feature-rich screenshot utility available in Windows 10. Snip & Sketch offers additional features, such as delay capture, ink effects, and integration with the Windows Ink Workspace, providing users with more flexibility and control over their screenshots. In addition to their individual features and capabilities, Paint and Snipping Tool can be used together to create and edit screenshots with annotations. For example, users can capture a screenshot using Snipping Tool, save it as an image file, and then open it in Paint to add annotations, such as arrows, text, and highlights, before saving or sharing the edited screenshot. Alternatively, users can use the "Copy" option in Snipping Tool to copy the screenshot to the clipboard and then paste it directly into Paint for editing. This allows users to combine the screenshotting capabilities of Snipping Tool with the drawing and editing tools of Paint to create customized and professional-looking screenshots for presentations, documentation, or communication purposes. Furthermore, both Paint and Snipping Tool support keyboard shortcuts for quick and efficient operation. For example, in Paint, users can press Ctrl + N to create a new blank canvas, Ctrl + O to open an existing image file, and Ctrl + S to save the current image. Similarly, in Snipping Tool, users can press Alt + N to start a new snip, Alt + D to delay a snip, and Ctrl + S to save the snip.

Overall, Paint and Snipping Tool are two indispensable applications that provide users with essential tools for creating, editing, and annotating images and screenshots in Windows. Whether performing basic image editing tasks, drawing diagrams, or capturing and annotating screenshots, these built-in Windows utilities offer users efficient and reliable solutions for a wide range of graphical needs. While Paint is ideal for drawing and editing images, Snipping Tool excels at capturing and annotating screenshots, making them a powerful combination for users who need to create and share visual content on a regular basis.

Chapter 6: Connecting to Networks and the Internet

Configuring Wi-Fi and Ethernet connections is essential for establishing network connectivity on a Windows-based system, enabling users to access the internet, share files and resources, and communicate with other devices on the network. In Windows, users can manage Wi-Fi and Ethernet connections through the Network and Sharing Center, accessible from the Control Panel or by clicking on the network icon in the system tray. From the Network and Sharing Center, users can view and manage their network connections, including Wi-Fi and Ethernet adapters, as well as configure network settings, such as IP address assignment, DNS server configuration, and network discovery. To configure a Wi-Fi connection in Windows, users can click on the Wi-Fi icon in the system tray, select the desired wireless network from the list of available networks, and enter the network security key if prompted. Alternatively, users can access Wi-Fi settings from the Network and Sharing Center, select "Set up a new connection or network," and choose "Connect to a wireless network" to manually add a Wi-Fi network by entering the network name (SSID) and security key. Moreover, users can view and manage their Wi-Fi network profiles by navigating to "Manage wireless networks" in the Network and Sharing Center, where they can delete saved network profiles, change network properties, or prioritize networks for automatic connection. Additionally, Windows provides command-line utilities, such as netsh and ipconfig, for configuring Wi-Fi and Ethernet connections from the Command Prompt. For example, users can use the "netsh wlan" command to view the list of available Wi-Fi networks, connect to a specific network, or export and import Wi-Fi profiles. Similarly, users can use the "ipconfig" command to view network configuration information, such as IP address, subnet mask, and default gateway, for both Wi-Fi and Ethernet connections. To configure an Ethernet connection in Windows, users can connect the Ethernet cable to the Ethernet port on the computer and the router or switch, and Windows will automatically detect and configure the connection. Alternatively, users can access Ethernet settings from the Network and Sharing Center, select "Set up a new connection or network," and choose "Connect to the Internet" to set up a wired (Ethernet) connection manually.

Moreover, users can view and manage their Ethernet network profiles by navigating to "Change adapter settings" in the Network and Sharing Center, where they can disable or enable Ethernet adapters, view connection status, or change adapter properties. Additionally, users can use command-line utilities, such as netsh and ipconfig, for configuring Ethernet connections from the Command Prompt. For example, users can use the "netsh interface" command to view the list of installed network adapters, enable or disable specific adapters, or configure advanced network settings, such as static IP addressing or VLAN tagging. Similarly, users can use the "ipconfig" command to renew the IP address, release the IP address, or flush the DNS resolver cache for Ethernet connections. Overall, configuring Wi-Fi and Ethernet connections in Windows is essential for establishing network connectivity and accessing network resources. Whether using the graphical user interface provided by the Network and Sharing Center or command-line utilities like netsh and ipconfig, users can easily configure and manage their network connections to ensure seamless communication and productivity. By understanding how to configure Wi-Fi and Ethernet connections in Windows, users can troubleshoot network issues, optimize network performance, and enhance their overall computing experience. Accessing shared files and printers on a network is fundamental for collaboration and resource sharing in a Windows-based environment, facilitating seamless communication and productivity among users across the network. In Windows, shared files and printers can be accessed through the network using the File Explorer and the Devices and Printers control panel, allowing users to browse, open, and manage shared resources from remote computers. To access shared files in Windows, users can open File Explorer and navigate to the "Network" section in the navigation pane, where they can view a list of available network locations and devices. From there, users can expand the network location corresponding to the desired computer or server to view shared folders and files. By double-clicking on a shared folder, users can access its contents and perform various file operations, such as opening, copying, moving, and deleting files. Additionally, users can map a network drive to a shared folder for easier access by right-clicking on the folder and selecting "Map network drive" from the context menu, or by clicking on the "Map network drive" button in the

File Explorer toolbar and specifying the drive letter and folder path. This creates a shortcut to the shared folder in File Explorer, allowing users to access it like a local drive. Moreover, users can use command-line utilities, such as net use and net view, for accessing shared files from the Command Prompt. For example, users can use the "net use" command to map a network drive to a shared folder by specifying the drive letter and UNC path. For instance, the command "net use Z: \server\share" maps the shared folder located on the server to drive Z: on the local computer. Similarly, users can use the "net view" command to list shared resources on a remote computer by specifying its hostname or IP address. This command displays a list of shared folders and printers available on the specified computer, allowing users to identify and access shared resources as needed. In addition to accessing shared files, users can also access shared printers on a network to print documents and other materials. To access shared printers in Windows, users can open the Devices and Printers control panel from the Start menu or by searching for "Devices and Printers" in the Windows search bar. From there, users can click on the "Add a printer" button to start the printer installation wizard and select "Add a network, wireless, or Bluetooth printer" to search for available printers on the network. Windows will then scan the network for shared printers and display a list of detected printers for users to choose from. By selecting a shared printer from the list and following the prompts to install the printer driver, users can add the shared printer to their list of available printers and start printing documents to it. Additionally, users can use command-line utilities, such as rundll32 and printui, for managing shared printers from the Command Prompt. For example, users can use the "rundll32 printui.dll,PrintUIEntry" command to open the Print Management console and add a shared printer by specifying its UNC path. This command launches the Add Printer wizard, where users can select the shared printer and install the necessary printer driver. Similarly, users can use the "printui /s /t2" command to display the Add Printer wizard in silent mode, allowing for automated printer installation without user intervention. In summary, accessing shared files and printers on a network is essential for collaboration and resource sharing in a Windows-based environment, enabling users to access remote resources and perform various file and print operations seamlessly. Whether using the graphical user interface provided by File Explorer and the Devices and Printers control panel or command-line utilities like net use and printui, users can easily access and manage shared resources on the network to enhance communication and productivity across the organization. By understanding how to access shared files and printers in Windows, users can leverage the power of network sharing to streamline workflows and improve efficiency in their daily tasks.

Chapter 7: Troubleshooting Common Windows Issues

Diagnosing and resolving startup problems in a Windows-based system is crucial for maintaining system stability and ensuring smooth operation. When a computer fails to start properly, it can be frustrating and disruptive, impacting productivity and workflow. However, with the right troubleshooting techniques and tools, many startup issues can be diagnosed and resolved effectively. One common startup problem in Windows is the failure to boot into the operating system, often indicated by error messages, system freezes, or infinite boot loops. To diagnose and resolve this issue, users can start by accessing the Advanced Startup Options menu, which provides various troubleshooting tools and options for repairing the system. To access the Advanced Startup Options menu, users can restart the computer and repeatedly press the F8 key or Shift + F8 key before the Windows logo appears during boot. Alternatively, users can use the Windows installation media or recovery drive to boot into the Advanced Startup Options menu. Once in the Advanced Startup Options menu, users can choose from various options, such as Safe Mode,

Startup Repair, System Restore, and Command Prompt, to diagnose and repair startup issues. For example, users can use Safe Mode to boot into Windows with a minimal set of drivers and services, allowing them to troubleshoot software-related issues that may be causing the startup problem. Users can also use Startup Repair to automatically fix common startup problems, such as missing or corrupted system files, by scanning the system and applying appropriate repairs. Moreover, users can use System Restore to revert the system to a previous state when it was working correctly, undoing any recent changes that may have caused the startup problem. Additionally, users can use the Command Prompt to run various diagnostic and repair commands to fix startup issues manually. For example, users can use the "chkdsk" command to check and repair disk errors, the "sfc /scannow" command to scan and repair system files, and the "bootrec" command to rebuild the Boot Configuration Data (BCD) store and repair the Master Boot Record (MBR) or Boot Sector. Another common startup problem in Windows is the presence of third-party software or drivers that conflict with the operating system or cause instability during boot. To diagnose and resolve this issue, users can boot into Safe Mode and uninstall recently installed software or drivers that may be causing the problem. Users can access Safe Mode by pressing the F8 key or Shift + F8 key during boot or using the Advanced Startup Options menu as described earlier. Once in Safe Mode, users can open the Control Panel, navigate to "Programs and Features" or "Device Manager," and uninstall any recently installed programs or drivers that may be causing the startup problem. Alternatively, users can use System Restore to revert the system to a previous state before the installation of problematic software or drivers. Moreover, users can use the System Configuration utility (msconfig) to perform a clean boot, disabling all non-essential startup items and services to isolate the cause of the problem. To perform a clean boot, users can open the System Configuration utility by typing "msconfig" in the Windows search bar and pressing Enter, selecting the "Selective startup" option on the General tab, and unchecking the "Load startup items" checkbox on the Services tab. This disables all non-essential startup items and services, allowing users to determine if a third-party program or service is causing the startup problem. In summary, diagnosing and resolving startup problems in a Windows-based system requires a systematic approach and the use of various troubleshooting tools and techniques. By accessing the Advanced Startup Options menu, performing diagnostic scans, using Safe Mode, and uninstalling problematic software or drivers, users can effectively diagnose and repair common startup issues, restoring system stability and ensuring smooth operation. By understanding how to diagnose and resolve startup problems in Windows, users can minimize downtime, improve system reliability, and maintain productivity in their computing environment. Fixing application crashes and freezes is essential for maintaining productivity and ensuring a smooth computing experience on a Windows-based system. When an application crashes or freezes, it can disrupt workflow and lead to data loss if not addressed promptly. However, with the right troubleshooting techniques and tools, many application issues can be diagnosed and resolved effectively.

One common cause of application crashes and freezes in Windows is corrupted or outdated software. To diagnose and resolve this issue, users can start by checking for updates to the affected application and installing any available updates. Many applications include built-in update mechanisms that allow users to download and install updates automatically. Alternatively, users can check the application's website or the Microsoft Store for updates and manually download and install them if necessary.

Another troubleshooting step is to check for system updates and install any available updates for Windows and other installed software. Outdated system components or drivers can sometimes cause compatibility issues that result in application crashes or freezes. Users can check for Windows updates by opening the Settings app, selecting "Update & Security," and clicking on "Check for updates." Additionally, users can check for driver updates using Device Manager or third-party driver update utilities.

If updating the application and system does not resolve the issue, users can try running the application in compatibility mode. Compatibility mode allows users to run older applications designed for previous versions of Windows on newer versions of the operating system. To run an application in compatibility mode, users can right-click on the application's shortcut or executable file, select "Properties," navigate to the "Compatibility" tab, and check the box next to "Run this program in compatibility mode for." Users can then select the desired version of Windows from the dropdown menu and click "Apply" to apply the changes.

Additionally, users can try running the application as an administrator to see if it resolves the issue. Running an application as an administrator grants it additional permissions and privileges that may be required to access certain system resources or perform certain operations. To run an application as an administrator, users can right-click on the application's shortcut or executable file, select "Run as administrator," and confirm the action if prompted by User Account Control (UAC).

If the application continues to crash or freeze, users can try resetting or reinstalling it to resolve any issues with its configuration or installation. Many applications include built-in repair or reset options that allow users to restore the application to its default settings without losing any data. Users can usually find these options in the application's settings or control panel. Alternatively, users can uninstall the application using the Control Panel or Settings app and then reinstall it from the original installation media or download it from the manufacturer's website.

In some cases, application crashes and freezes may be caused by underlying system issues, such as corrupted system files or hardware problems. To diagnose and resolve these issues, users can use built-in Windows troubleshooting tools, such as the System File Checker (sfc) and the

Deployment Image Servicing and Management (DISM) tool. The System File Checker scans the system for corrupted or missing system files and repairs them automatically. Users can run the System File Checker by opening an elevated Command Prompt and running the command "sfc /scannow." Similarly, the DISM tool checks the integrity of the Windows image and repairs any issues it finds. Users can run the DISM tool by opening an elevated Command Prompt and running the command "dism /online /cleanup-image /restorehealth."

Another troubleshooting step is to check for overheating or hardware issues that may be causing the application to crash or freeze. Overheating can cause the system to become unstable and may lead to crashes or freezes when running demanding applications. Users can monitor the system's temperature using third-party monitoring utilities or the built-in Windows Task Manager. Additionally, users can check for hardware issues by running diagnostic tests using built-in or third-party hardware diagnostic tools.

In summary, fixing application crashes and freezes in Windows requires a systematic approach and the use of various troubleshooting techniques and tools. By updating the application and system, running the application in compatibility mode or as an administrator, resetting or reinstalling the application, and diagnosing and resolving underlying system or hardware issues, users can effectively diagnose and resolve common application problems, restoring stability and ensuring a smooth computing experience. By understanding how to troubleshoot application crashes and freezes in Windows, users can minimize downtime, improve system reliability, and maintain productivity in their computing environment.

Chapter 8: Advanced Tips and Tricks for Power Users

Command Prompt (CMD) is a powerful tool in Windows that allows users to interact with the operating system using text-based commands, offering a range of tricks and shortcuts to enhance productivity and efficiency. One useful trick is the ability to navigate through directories quickly using keyboard shortcuts. For instance, users can use the "cd" command followed by a directory path to change directories. To navigate up one directory level, users can type "cd.." and press Enter. To navigate to the root directory, users can type "cd" and press Enter. Additionally, users can use the Tab key to autocomplete directory and file names, reducing the need for manual typing. Another useful trick is the ability to view the contents of a directory in a hierarchical tree structure using the "tree" command. By typing "tree" followed by a directory path and pressing Enter, users can see a visual representation of the directory structure, making it easier to understand the organization of files and folders. Furthermore, users can customize the appearance of the Command Prompt window to suit their preferences. For example, users can change the text and background colors, adjust the font size and style, and enable or disable transparency. To customize the Command Prompt window, users can right-click on the title bar, select "Properties," and navigate to the "Colors" and "Font" tabs to make the desired changes. Additionally, users can resize the Command Prompt window by dragging the edges with the mouse or using keyboard shortcuts. To maximize the window, users can press Alt + Enter, and to resize it to a specific size, users can use the "mode" command followed by the desired width and height values. Another helpful trick is the ability to copy and paste text within the Command Prompt window. While the traditional method of copying and pasting using Ctrl + C and Ctrl + V works in most cases, users can also use the keyboard shortcuts Alt + Space, E, and P to access the Edit menu and paste text from the clipboard. Moreover, users can use the "clip" command to copy the output of a command to the clipboard directly. For example, users can type a command followed by "| clip" to copy the output to the clipboard without displaying it in the Command Prompt window. Additionally, users can create and run batch files to automate repetitive tasks and execute multiple commands sequentially. To create a batch file, users can open

Notepad, type the desired commands, and save the file with a .bat extension. To run a batch file, users can simply double-click on the file, or they can run it from the Command Prompt by typing the file path and pressing Enter. Furthermore, users can use the "start" command followed by a program name to launch applications directly from the Command Prompt. For instance, users can type "start notepad" to open Notepad or "start chrome" to launch Google Chrome. Moreover, users can use keyboard shortcuts to perform common tasks quickly. For example, users can press Ctrl + C to interrupt a running command, Ctrl + Break to stop a command permanently, and Ctrl + D to close the Command Prompt window. Additionally, users can use the arrow keys to navigate through previously executed commands, making it easy to repeat or edit commands as needed. Furthermore, users can use the "cls" command to clear the contents of the Command Prompt window, providing a clean slate for entering new commands. Another useful trick is the ability to access a list of previously executed commands using the F7 key. By pressing F7, users can see a list of recent commands and select one to execute again. Moreover, users can use the "assoc" and "ftype" commands to view and modify file associations in

Windows. The "assoc" command displays a list of file extensions and their associated file types, while the "ftype" command displays a list of file types and the commands used to open them. For example, users can use the "assoc .txt" command to view the file association for .txt files, and the "ftype txtfile" command to view the command used to open .txt files. Additionally, users can use the "title" command to set a custom title for the Command Prompt window, making it easier to identify when working with multiple windows. For example, users can type "title My Command Prompt" to set the title of the window to "My Command Prompt." Furthermore, users can use the "prompt" command to customize the command prompt text, adding information such as the current directory, date, time, or username. For example, users can type "prompt PG" to display the current directory followed by a greater than sign. In summary, Command Prompt offers a range of tricks and shortcuts to enhance productivity and efficiency in Windows. By mastering these tricks and shortcuts, users can navigate directories quickly, customize the appearance of the Command Prompt window, copy and paste text efficiently, automate tasks with batch files, and perform common tasks with keyboard shortcuts. Whether managing files and directories, executing commands, or customizing the Command Prompt environment, these tricks and shortcuts empower users to work more effectively and efficiently in Windows. Registry hacks and system tweaks are powerful tools for customizing and optimizing a Windows-based system, allowing users to modify various settings and behaviors to better suit their preferences and needs. The Windows Registry is a hierarchical database that stores configuration settings and options for the operating system and installed applications, and making changes to the registry can alter how the system operates. However, it's important to note that modifying the registry can have unintended consequences if done incorrectly, so it's essential to proceed with caution and create a backup of the registry before making any changes.

One common registry hack is the ability to customize the Windows Explorer context menu, which appears when right-clicking on files, folders, or the desktop. By adding or removing items from the context menu, users can streamline their workflow and access frequently used actions more quickly. To customize the context menu, users can navigate to the appropriate registry key using the Registry Editor, which can be accessed by typing "regedit" in the Run dialog box or the

Command Prompt and pressing Enter. Once in the Registry Editor, users can navigate to the "HKEY_CLASSES_ROOT* \shell" key to customize the context menu for files or the "HKEY_CLASSES_ROOT\Directory\shell" key to customize the context menu for folders. From there, users can add new subkeys to create custom context menu items or delete existing subkeys to remove unwanted items. It's essential to be careful when editing the registry, as deleting or modifying the wrong keys can cause system instability or even prevent Windows from booting. Another useful registry tweak is the ability to customize the appearance and behavior of the Taskbar and Start menu. By modifying registry keys related to the Taskbar and Start menu, users can change various settings, such as the size and position of the Taskbar, the appearance of Taskbar buttons, and the behavior of the Start menu. For example, users can navigate to the "HKEY_CURRENT_USER\Software\Microsoft\Windows\CurrentVersion\Explorer\Advanced" key to modify settings such as Taskbar size, Taskbar animations, and Start menu behavior. Again, it's important to exercise caution when editing the registry, as incorrect changes can have unintended consequences.

Additionally, users can tweak various system settings and behaviors by modifying registry keys related to system performance, network settings, and user interface customization. For example, users can navigate to the "HKEY_LOCAL_MACHINE\SYSTEM\CurrentControl Set\Services\Tcpip\Parameters" key to modify TCP/IP settings such as TCP window size, Maximum Transmission Unit (MTU), and Time to Live (TTL). Similarly, users can navigate to the "HKEY_CURRENT_USER\Control Panel\Desktop" key to customize settings such as desktop background, screensaver, and keyboard shortcuts. By making strategic changes to these registry keys, users can enhance system performance, improve network connectivity, and personalize the user experience.

Furthermore, users can create and apply registry tweaks using registry files (.reg), which contain a collection of registry keys and values that can be imported into the registry with a double-click. To create a registry file, users can open Notepad, enter the desired registry keys and values in the following format:

csharpCopy code

```
Windows Registry Editor Version 5.00
[HKEY_CURRENT_USER\Software\Microsoft\Wind
```

ows\CurrentVersion\Explorer\Advanced]
"EnableBalloonTips"=dword:00000000

Once the desired registry keys and values have been entered, users can save the file with a .reg extension and double-click it to import the changes into the registry. It's important to verify the contents of the registry file before importing it to ensure that it contains only the desired changes.

Moreover, users can tweak system settings and behaviors using Command Prompt commands and scripts. For example, users can use the "reg add" command to add new registry keys and values, the "reg delete" command to delete existing registry keys and values, and the "reg query" command to view the contents of registry keys. Additionally, users can create batch scripts (.bat) containing a series of Command Prompt commands to automate the process of applying registry tweaks. By running these scripts, users can quickly and efficiently apply multiple registry tweaks at once.

In summary, registry hacks and system tweaks are powerful tools for customizing and optimizing a Windows-based system, allowing users to modify various settings and behaviors to better suit their preferences and needs. Whether customizing the Windows Explorer context menu, tweaking

Taskbar and Start menu settings, or modifying system performance and network settings, registry hacks and system tweaks empower users to take control of their computing environment and enhance their overall user experience. However, it's important to exercise caution when editing the registry and to create backups before making any changes to avoid unintended consequences. With careful planning and execution, users can leverage registry hacks and system tweaks to unlock the full potential of their Windows-based system.

BOOK 2

LINUX UNLEASHED
FROM NOVICE TO SYSTEM ADMINISTRATOR

ROB BOTWRIGHT

Chapter 1: Introduction to Linux: The Basics

The history and philosophy of Linux provide a fascinating insight into the evolution and principles behind one of the most influential operating systems in the world. Linux, born out of the personal passion and ingenuity of Linus Torvalds in 1991, emerged as a Unix-like operating system built on open-source principles. At its core, Linux embodies the collaborative spirit of the open-source community, where developers from around the world contribute their expertise to create a free and accessible operating system for everyone. The story of Linux begins with Linus Torvalds, a Finnish computer science student who set out to create a Unix-like operating system that he could run on his personal computer. Frustrated by the limitations of existing operating systems and inspired by the ideals of open-source software, Torvalds began work on what would eventually become the Linux kernel. In August 1991, Torvalds released the first version of the Linux kernel to the world, inviting other developers to contribute to its development. From its humble beginnings as a hobby project, Linux quickly gained traction among developers and enthusiasts, who were drawn to its flexibility, stability, and performance. One of the defining characteristics of Linux is its open-source nature, which allows anyone to view, modify, and distribute the source code freely. This openness fosters innovation and collaboration, as developers can build upon each other's work and contribute improvements back to the community. The Linux philosophy is rooted in the principles of freedom, collaboration, and transparency. Unlike proprietary operating systems, which are developed and controlled by a single company, Linux is a community-driven project with no single owner or corporation. This decentralized model ensures that Linux remains free from the constraints of corporate interests and empowers users to take control of their computing experience. Central to the Linux philosophy is the concept of "free software," which refers to software that respects users' freedom and allows them to run, study, modify, and distribute it as they see fit. The Free Software Foundation, founded by Richard Stallman in 1985, has been a driving force behind the free software movement and has played a significant role in shaping the philosophy of Linux. Linux distributions, or "distros," play a crucial role in the Linux ecosystem, providing users with a complete operating system that includes the Linux kernel, system utilities, and software packages. There are hundreds of Linux distributions available, each tailored to specific use cases and user preferences. Some popular Linux distributions include Ubuntu, Debian, Fedora, and CentOS, each with its own community of developers and users. One of the key benefits of Linux is its versatility and adaptability, which allows it to run on a wide range of hardware platforms, from desktop computers and servers to embedded systems and supercomputers. This versatility has made Linux the operating system of choice for a variety of applications, including web hosting, cloud computing, scientific research, and mobile devices. Moreover, Linux has gained widespread adoption in the enterprise sector, where its stability, security, and cost-effectiveness make it an attractive alternative to proprietary operating systems. Over the years, Linux has continued to evolve and grow, driven by the passion and dedication of its community of developers and users. From its humble beginnings as a personal project to its current status as a global phenomenon, Linux remains a testament to the power of collaboration, innovation, and freedom in the world of technology. As Linux continues to evolve and shape the future of computing, its history and philosophy serve as a reminder of the values that have guided its development and the principles that continue to drive its success. Whether you're a seasoned Linux user or new to the world of open-source software, understanding the history and philosophy of Linux is essential for appreciating its impact and significance in the world of technology. By embracing the spirit of collaboration, openness, and innovation that defines Linux, we can all play a part in shaping the future of computing for generations to come.

Understanding Linux distributions is essential for anyone looking to explore the world of Linux and harness its power for various computing needs. A Linux distribution, often referred to as a "distro," is a complete operating system built around the Linux kernel and bundled with a collection of software packages, system utilities, and user interfaces. These distributions vary widely in terms of features, performance, and target use cases, catering to the diverse needs and preferences of users. One of the most popular and widely used Linux distributions is Ubuntu, known for its user-friendly interface, robust security features, and extensive software repositories. Ubuntu is based on Debian, another prominent Linux distribution known for its stability, reliability, and commitment to free and open-source software. Debian serves as the foundation for many other Linux distributions, providing a solid framework for building custom solutions and specialized distributions tailored to specific use cases. Another popular Linux distribution is Fedora, sponsored by Red Hat, Inc., and known for its cutting-edge features, frequent updates, and strong focus on innovation. Fedora serves as a testing ground for new technologies and features that eventually find their way into other Linux distributions, making it a favorite among developers and enthusiasts. CentOS is another notable Linux distribution, derived from the same upstream sources as Red Hat Enterprise Linux (RHEL) and known for its stability, long-term support, and suitability for enterprise environments. CentOS is often used in production servers and critical infrastructure where reliability and security are paramount. Moreover, there are specialized Linux distributions designed for specific use cases, such as Kali Linux for penetration testing and security auditing, Arch Linux for advanced users seeking a minimalist and customizable system, and Raspbian for the Raspberry Pi single-board computer. Each Linux distribution comes with its package management system, which allows users to install, update, and manage software packages conveniently. One of the most common package management systems in Linux is APT (Advanced Package Tool), used by Debian-based distributions such as Ubuntu and Debian. With APT, users can install software packages from repositories using commands such as "sudo apt-get install [package-name]" and update the package cache using "sudo apt-get update." Another popular package management system is YUM (Yellowdog Updater, Modified), used by Red Hat-based distributions such as Fedora and CentOS. With YUM, users can install software packages using commands such as "sudo yum install [package-name]" and update the package cache using "sudo yum update." Additionally, Linux distributions offer various desktop environments, which provide graphical user interfaces (GUIs) for interacting with the operating system and applications. Some common desktop environments include GNOME, KDE Plasma, Xfce, and LXQt, each with its unique look, feel, and features. Users can choose their preferred desktop environment during the installation process or install additional desktop environments later using package management tools. Furthermore, Linux distributions often come with pre-installed software applications, including web browsers, office suites, multimedia players, and development tools. However, users can install additional software packages from repositories to customize their system according to their needs and preferences. Linux distributions are also known for their strong security features, including user permissions, access controls, and encryption mechanisms. By default, Linux enforces a robust system of user permissions, which restricts access to system resources and protects against unauthorized actions. Users can create multiple user accounts with different privileges and assign permissions to files and directories using commands such as "chmod" and "chown." Additionally, Linux distributions offer built-in firewall utilities, such as iptables and firewalld, which allow users to control network traffic and block malicious connections. Moreover, Linux distributions support full disk encryption, which encrypts data at rest to protect it from unauthorized access. Users can encrypt their entire disk during the installation process or encrypt specific partitions using tools such as LUKS (Linux Unified Key Setup) and dm-crypt. In summary, Linux distributions offer a diverse and flexible ecosystem of operating systems tailored to various needs and preferences. Whether you're a beginner looking for a user-friendly desktop environment, a developer seeking cutting-edge features, or a sysadmin managing enterprise servers, there's a Linux distribution out there for you. By understanding the different features, package management systems, desktop environments, and security mechanisms offered by Linux distributions, users can make informed decisions and leverage the power of Linux to its fullest potential.

Chapter 2: Getting Started with the Command Line Interface

The introduction to shell and terminal is fundamental for anyone delving into the world of Unix-like operating systems, offering a powerful and efficient means of interacting with the underlying system through text-based commands. At its core, the shell is a command-line interpreter that allows users to execute commands, run scripts, and manipulate files and directories using a textual interface. The terminal, on the other hand, is the application that provides access to the shell, allowing users to input commands and view their output in a text-based environment. One of the most commonly used shells in Unix-like operating systems is the Bourne Again Shell (bash), which is the default shell for many Linux distributions and macOS. Bash offers a wide range of features, including command-line editing, tab completion, and shell scripting capabilities, making it a versatile and powerful tool for both novice and experienced users. To open a terminal window and start using the bash shell, users can simply launch the terminal application from their desktop environment or use the keyboard shortcut Ctrl + Alt + T. Once the terminal window is open, users can start typing commands and pressing Enter to execute them. For example, users can type "ls" to list the contents of the current directory, "cd" to change directories, and "mkdir" to create a new directory. Moreover, users can use command-line options and arguments to modify the behavior of commands and achieve specific tasks. For instance, users can use the "-l" option with the "ls" command to display detailed information about files and directories, or the "-r" option with the "rm" command to remove files and directories recursively. Additionally, users can use wildcards, such as "" and "?", to match multiple files and directories based on patterns or criteria. For example, users can use the "" wildcard to match all files and directories in a directory, or the "?" wildcard to match a single character. Furthermore, users can use pipes ("|") to combine multiple commands and redirect the output of one command as the input to another. For example, users can use the "ls" command to list files and directories and pipe the output to the "grep" command to search for specific files or patterns. Similarly, users can use the ">" and ">>" operators to redirect the output of a command to a file, with ">" overwriting the contents of the file and ">>" appending the output to the end of the file. Another useful feature of the shell is shell scripting, which allows users to automate repetitive tasks and create custom solutions using shell scripts. Shell scripts are text files containing a series of shell commands and instructions that are executed sequentially by the shell. To create a shell script, users can open a text editor such as nano or vi, write the desired commands and instructions, and save the file with a ".sh" extension. Once the shell script is saved, users can make it executable using the "chmod" command and run it like any other executable file. For example, users can use the command "chmod +x script.sh" to make the script executable and "./script.sh" to run it. Moreover, users can use environment variables to store and retrieve information within shell scripts, allowing for greater flexibility and customization. Environment variables are variables that hold information about the environment in which the shell is running, such as the user's home directory, the current working directory, and the system architecture. Users can set environment variables using the "export" command and retrieve their values using the "$" prefix. For example, users can use the command "export MY_VAR=value" to set the environment variable "MY_VAR" to "value" and "echo $MY_VAR" to retrieve its value. Additionally, users can use conditional statements, loops, and functions in shell scripts to create more complex and sophisticated solutions. Conditional statements, such as "if" and "case," allow users to execute commands based on certain conditions or criteria, while loops, such as "for" and "while," allow users to execute commands repeatedly until a certain condition is met. Functions, on the other hand, allow users to encapsulate a series of commands and instructions into a reusable block of code. In summary, the shell and terminal provide a powerful and efficient means of interacting with Unix-like operating systems through text-based commands. By mastering the basics of the shell, including command-line navigation, command execution, shell scripting, and environment variables, users can unlock the full potential of their system and streamline their workflow. Whether performing simple file manipulations, automating repetitive tasks, or creating custom solutions, the shell and terminal offer a versatile and flexible environment for users to work and innovate.

Understanding the basic command structure and usage is fundamental for navigating and interacting with the command-line interface (CLI) effectively in Unix-like operating systems. In the CLI, commands are the primary means of performing various tasks, such as managing files and directories, configuring system settings, and executing programs. Each command follows a specific structure, typically consisting of the command name, options, and arguments. The command name identifies the action to be performed, while options modify the behavior of the command, and arguments provide additional information or specify the target of the command. For example, the "ls" command is used to list the contents of a directory, and its basic structure is "ls [options] [arguments]." By default, the "ls" command lists the contents of the current directory without any options or arguments. However, users can customize the behavior of the "ls" command by adding options such as "-l" to display detailed information about files and directories or "-a" to include hidden files and directories in the output. Additionally, users can specify the target directory as an argument to the "ls" command to list the contents of a specific directory rather than the current directory. Similarly, other commands follow a similar structure, with variations in the command name, options, and arguments depending on the specific task to be performed. For example, the "mkdir" command is used to create a new directory, and its basic structure is "mkdir [options] [directory]." Users can specify options such as "-p" to create parent directories if they do not exist or "-m" to set the permissions of the newly created directory. Additionally, users can specify the name of the directory to be created as an argument to the "mkdir" command. Moreover, commands can be chained together using pipes ("|") to perform more complex operations or achieve specific tasks. Pipes allow the output of one command to be used as the input to another command, enabling users to combine multiple commands into a single operation. For example, the "ls" command can be piped to the "grep" command to search for files or directories matching a specific pattern, or the "find" command can be piped to the "xargs" command to perform actions on the results of the find operation. Additionally, commands can be executed in the background by appending an ampersand ("&") to the end of the command. This allows users to continue working in the CLI while the command is running in the background. For example, the "sleep" command can be used to pause execution for a specified period of time, and appending "&" to the end of the command allows users to continue working while the sleep command is running. Furthermore, users can create aliases for frequently used commands to simplify their usage and improve productivity. Aliases are custom shortcuts that allow users to define alternative names for commands or command sequences. Users can define aliases using the "alias" command followed by the desired alias name and command sequence. For example, users can create an alias named "ll" for the "ls -l" command by running "alias ll='ls -l'." Once defined, users can use the alias "ll" to list the contents of a directory in long format, saving time and keystrokes. Additionally, users can customize their command-line prompt to provide valuable information and improve usability. The command-line prompt, also known as the shell prompt, is displayed before each command and typically includes information such as the username, hostname, current working directory, and timestamp. Users can customize the prompt using escape sequences and environment variables to display the desired information in the desired format. For example, users can customize the prompt to display the current username and hostname followed by the current working directory and a timestamp. In summary, mastering the basic command structure and usage is essential for effectively navigating and interacting with the command-line interface in Unix-like operating systems. By understanding the structure of commands, including the command name, options, and arguments, users can perform a wide range of tasks efficiently and confidently. Additionally, by learning advanced techniques such as command chaining, background execution, aliases, and prompt customization, users can further enhance their productivity and streamline their workflow in the CLI.

Chapter 3: Understanding File System Navigation and Manipulation

The file system hierarchy in Linux provides a structured organization of files and directories, essential for managing and accessing data efficiently within the operating system. At the root of the file system hierarchy is the root directory, represented by a forward slash ("/"), which serves as the starting point for navigating the entire file system. The root directory contains essential system files and directories, including system binaries, device files, and configuration files, necessary for the operation of the operating system. One of the fundamental directories in the Linux file system hierarchy is the "/bin" directory, which contains essential system binaries and commands required for basic system functionality. Commands such as "ls," "cp," and "mkdir" are located in the "/bin" directory, allowing users to perform common tasks without specifying the full path to the command. Similarly, the "/sbin" directory contains system binaries and commands used for system administration tasks, such as managing network interfaces, disk partitions, and system services. Commands such as "ifconfig," "fdisk," and "iptables" are located in the "/sbin" directory, typically requiring administrative privileges to execute. Moreover, the "/usr" directory contains user-related files and directories, including user binaries, libraries, documentation, and shared resources. The "/usr/bin" directory contains user binaries and commands installed by the system administrator or package manager, while the "/usr/lib" directory contains shared libraries used by applications and system services. Additionally, the "/usr/share" directory contains shared resources such as documentation, icons, and locale files, accessible to all users on the system. Another essential directory in the Linux file system hierarchy is the "/etc" directory, which contains system-wide configuration files and settings used by the operating system and installed applications. Configuration files for various system services, such as networking, user authentication, and package management, are located in the "/etc" directory, allowing administrators to customize system behavior and settings. For example, the "/etc/network/interfaces" file contains network interface configuration settings, while the "/etc/passwd" and "/etc/group" files contain user account information and group membership information, respectively. Furthermore, the "/var" directory contains variable data files and directories, including system logs, temporary files, and spool directories, which change frequently during system operation. System log files generated by system services and applications are stored in the "/var/log" directory, allowing administrators to monitor system activity and diagnose problems. Temporary files created by applications and users are stored in the "/var/tmp" directory, while print job files and mail spools are stored in the "/var/spool" directory. Additionally, the "/home" directory contains user home directories, where user-specific files and settings are stored. Each user on the system has a unique home directory located within the "/home" directory, typically named after their username. User configuration files, personal documents, and other user-specific data are stored in the user's home directory, providing a private space for each user to work and store their files. Another important directory in the Linux file system hierarchy is the "/tmp" directory, which contains temporary files and directories created by the system and users. Temporary files created by applications and system services are stored in the "/tmp" directory, allowing for temporary storage of data without affecting other files or directories on the system. Users can also create temporary files and directories in the "/tmp" directory for their use, but these files are typically deleted automatically when the system reboots. Additionally, the "/boot" directory contains files and directories related to the system boot process, including boot loader configuration files, kernel images, and initial ramdisk files. The boot loader configuration file, typically named "grub.cfg" or "menu.lst," is located in the "/boot/grub" directory and contains settings and options for booting the operating system. Kernel images and initial ramdisk files, necessary for booting the system, are stored in the "/boot" directory, allowing the system to load the necessary components during the boot process. In summary, the file system hierarchy in Linux provides a structured organization of files and directories, essential for managing and accessing data efficiently within the operating system. By understanding the purpose and function of each directory in the file system hierarchy, administrators and users can navigate the file system effectively, customize system settings, and manage files and directories according to their needs.

Working with directories and files is a fundamental aspect of managing data and organizing content in any operating system, including Unix-like systems such as Linux. Directories, also known as folders, serve as containers for storing files and other directories, allowing users to organize and structure their data in a hierarchical manner. The "mkdir" command is commonly used to create directories in the command-line interface (CLI). By typing "mkdir" followed by the name of the directory to be created, users can quickly and easily create new directories. For example, to create a directory named "documents," users can type "mkdir documents" in the CLI. Additionally, users can create directories with multiple levels of nesting by specifying the "-p" option with the "mkdir" command. This option allows users to create parent directories if they do not already exist. For example, to create a directory named "photos" inside a directory named "vacation" inside a directory named "2024," users can type "mkdir -p 2024/vacation/photos" in the CLI. Once directories are created, users can navigate between directories using the "cd" command. The "cd" command stands for "change directory" and is used to switch the current working directory to another directory. For example, to change the current working directory to the "documents" directory created earlier, users can type "cd documents" in the CLI. Moreover, users can use relative and absolute paths with the "cd" command to navigate to directories located at different levels in the file system hierarchy. Relative paths specify the location of a directory relative to the current working directory, while absolute paths specify the full path to the directory from the root directory. For example, to navigate to the "photos" directory inside the "vacation" directory, users can type "cd vacation/photos" for relative path navigation or "cd /path/to/vacation/photos" for absolute path navigation. Once inside a directory, users can perform various operations on files and directories, such as creating, copying, moving, and deleting them. The "touch" command is commonly used to create empty files in the CLI. By typing "touch" followed by the name of the file to be created, users can create new files quickly and easily. For example, to create a file named "notes.txt," users can type "touch notes.txt" in the CLI. Additionally, users can create multiple files simultaneously by specifying multiple file names separated by spaces. For example, to create files named "file1.txt," "file2.txt," and "file3.txt," users can type "touch file1.txt file2.txt file3.txt" in the CLI. Moreover, users can copy files and directories from one location to another using the "cp" command. The "cp" command stands for "copy" and is used to copy files and directories from a source location to a destination location. For example, to copy a file named "source.txt" to a directory named "destination," users can type "cp source.txt destination" in the CLI. Additionally, users can use the "-r" option with the "cp" command to copy directories and their contents recursively. For example, to copy a directory named "source" to a directory named "destination," users can type "cp -r source destination" in the CLI. Furthermore, users can move files and directories from one location to another using the "mv" command. The "mv" command stands for "move" and is used to move files and directories from a source location to a destination location. For example, to move a file named "source.txt" to a directory named "destination," users can type "mv source.txt destination" in the CLI. Additionally, users can use the "mv" command to rename files and directories by specifying a different name for the destination. For example, to rename a file named "source.txt" to "destination.txt," users can type "mv source.txt destination.txt" in the CLI. Moreover, users can delete files and directories using the "rm" command. The "rm" command stands for "remove" and is used to delete files and directories from the file system. For example, to delete a file named "file.txt," users can type "rm file.txt" in the CLI. Additionally, users can use the "-r" option with the "rm" command to delete directories and their contents recursively. For example, to delete a directory named "directory" and all its contents, users can type "rm -r directory" in the CLI. In summary, working with directories and files is an essential skill for managing data and organizing content in Unix-like operating systems such as Linux. By mastering basic CLI commands for creating, navigating, copying, moving, and deleting directories and files, users can efficiently manage their data and streamline their workflow in the command-line interface.

Chapter 4: Mastering File Permissions and Ownership

Understanding Linux file permissions is crucial for users and administrators to effectively manage access to files and directories within the system. In Linux, each file and directory has associated permissions that define who can read, write, or execute them. These permissions are represented by a set of nine characters, organized into three groups of three: user, group, and others. The "ls -l" command is commonly used to display file permissions in the CLI. When executed, this command lists detailed information about files and directories in the current directory, including their permissions, owner, group, size, and modification date. The first column of the output represents the file type and permissions, displayed as a combination of nine characters. The first character indicates the file type, with "-" representing a regular file and "d" representing a directory. The next three characters represent the permissions for the file owner, specifying whether the owner has read, write, or execute permissions. The characters "r," "w," and "x" represent read, write, and execute permissions, respectively, while "-" indicates no permission. For example, "rwx" indicates read, write, and execute permissions, "rw-" indicates read and write permissions only, and "---" indicates no permissions. The next three characters represent the permissions for the group associated with the file, following the same format as the user permissions. Finally, the last three characters represent the permissions for all other users on the system, also following the same format. To modify file permissions, users can use the "chmod" command in the CLI. The "chmod" command allows users to change the permissions of files and directories by specifying the desired permissions and the target file or directory. Permissions can be expressed using symbolic notation, where "u" represents the user, "g" represents the group, and "o" represents others, followed by "+", "-", or "=" to add, remove, or set permissions, respectively. For example, to give the owner of a file read and write permissions, users can type "chmod u+rw filename" in the CLI. Additionally, permissions can be expressed using octal notation, where each permission is represented by a three-bit binary number, with "4" representing read, "2" representing write, and "1" representing execute. Users can calculate the octal value for desired permissions and specify it directly with the "chmod" command. For example, to give the owner of a file read, write, and execute permissions, users can type "chmod 700 filename" in the CLI. Moreover, users can change the ownership of files and directories using the "chown" command in the CLI. The "chown" command allows users to change the owner and group associated with a file or directory by specifying the new owner and group. For example, to change the owner of a file named "file.txt" to a user named "user," users can type "chown user file.txt" in the CLI. Additionally, users can specify both the new owner and group by separating them with a colon ":". For example, to change the owner and group of a file named "file.txt" to a user named "user" and a group named "group," users can type "chown user:group file.txt" in the CLI. Furthermore, users can use the "chgrp" command to change the group associated with a file or directory without changing the owner. The "chgrp" command allows users to specify the new group and the target file or directory. For example, to change the group of a file named "file.txt" to a group named "group," users can type "chgrp group file.txt" in the CLI. In summary, understanding Linux file permissions is essential for managing access to files and directories within the system effectively. By learning how to interpret file permissions, modify them using the "chmod" command, and change ownership and group associations using the "chown" and "chgrp" commands, users and administrators can ensure the security and integrity of their data and maintain control over access to sensitive information. Changing file permissions and ownership is a crucial aspect of managing files and directories in Unix-like operating systems such as Linux. Permissions control who can read, write, or execute files and directories, while ownership determines which user and group have control over them. Users can modify permissions and ownership using various CLI commands, such as "chmod," "chown," and "chgrp." The "chmod" command allows users to change file permissions, granting or revoking read, write, and execute permissions for the file owner, group, and others. Permissions can be expressed using symbolic notation, where "u" represents the user, "g" represents the group, and "o" represents others, followed by "+", "-", or "=" to add, remove, or set permissions, respectively. For instance, to give the owner read and write permissions for a file named "example.txt," users can type "chmod u+rw example.txt" in the CLI. Alternatively, permissions can be specified using octal notation, where each permission is represented by a three-bit binary number. For example, to set read, write, and execute permissions for the owner and read-only permissions for the group and others, users can type "chmod 755 example.txt." Furthermore, users can change file ownership using the "chown" command, allowing them to transfer ownership from one user to another. Users can specify the new owner by providing the username or user ID along with the target file or directory. For instance, to change the owner of a file named "example.txt" to a user named "john," users can type "chown john example.txt" in the CLI. Additionally, users can change both the owner and group simultaneously by separating them with a colon ":". For example, to change both the owner and group of "example.txt" to "john" and "developers," respectively, users can type "chown john:developers example.txt." Similarly, the "chgrp" command allows users to change the group associated with a file or directory without changing the owner. Users can specify the new group by providing the group name or group ID along with the target file or directory. For example, to change the group of "example.txt" to a group named "staff," users can type "chgrp staff example.txt" in the CLI. Additionally, users can use symbolic links to change permissions and ownership indirectly. Symbolic links, also known as symlinks or soft links, are special files that point to another file or directory. By creating a symbolic link, users can manipulate permissions and ownership for the link itself rather than the target file or directory. However, changes made to the link do not affect the target file or directory. To create a symbolic link, users can use the "ln -s" command followed by the target file or directory and the name of the link. For instance, to create a symbolic link named "link.txt" that points to "example.txt," users can type "ln -s example.txt link.txt" in the CLI. Once the link is created, users can modify its permissions and ownership using the aforementioned commands. Moreover, users can use the "sudo" command to change permissions and ownership for files and directories that require elevated privileges. The "sudo" command allows users to execute commands with superuser or root privileges, enabling them to perform administrative tasks such as changing permissions and ownership. For example, to change permissions for a system configuration file that requires root privileges, users can type "sudo chmod 644 config.txt" in the CLI. Similarly, users can use "sudo" with "chown" and "chgrp" to change ownership and group membership for system files and directories. In summary, changing file permissions and ownership is a fundamental aspect of managing files and directories in Unix-like operating systems. By understanding how to use commands such as "chmod," "chown," and "chgrp," users can control access to their files and directories, ensuring security and integrity within the system. Additionally, symbolic links and the "sudo" command provide additional flexibility and capabilities for managing permissions and ownership, allowing users to perform administrative tasks effectively.

Chapter 5: Configuring and Managing User Accounts

Creating and managing user accounts is a fundamental aspect of system administration in Unix-like operating systems such as Linux. User accounts allow individuals to access the system, perform tasks, and customize their computing environment according to their preferences and requirements. The "adduser" command is commonly used to create new user accounts in the command-line interface (CLI). By typing "adduser" followed by the username of the new user, users can initiate the process of creating a new user account. For example, to create a new user account named "john," users can type "adduser john" in the CLI. Upon executing the command, users will be prompted to enter additional information for the new user, such as their full name, room number, and phone number. After providing the required information, the "adduser" command will create a new user account with default settings, including a home directory and a unique user ID (UID). Additionally, users can specify various options with the "adduser" command to customize the behavior of the new user account. For example, the "-m" option can be used to create a home directory for the new user, ensuring that they have a dedicated space for storing personal files and configurations. To add a new user account with a home directory, users can type "adduser -m john" in the CLI. Moreover, users can use the "useradd" command to create new user accounts directly from the CLI. Similar to the "adduser" command, the "useradd" command allows users to specify various options and parameters to customize the behavior of the new user account. For example, to create a new user account named "jane" with a specific UID and primary group, users can type "useradd -u 1001 -g users jane" in the CLI. Upon executing the command, the "useradd" command will create a new user account with the specified UID and primary group, but without a home directory. To create a home directory for the new user, users can use the "-m" option with the "useradd" command, similar to the "adduser" command. Another important aspect of managing user accounts is setting passwords for user authentication. The "passwd" command is used to set or change passwords for user accounts in the CLI. By typing "passwd" followed by the username of the target user, users can initiate the process of setting or changing the password for the specified user account. For example, to set or change the password for the user account "john," users can type "passwd john" in the CLI. Upon executing the command, users will be prompted to enter and confirm the new password for the specified user account. After successfully setting or changing the password, the "passwd" command will update the password database accordingly. Additionally, users can use various options with the "passwd" command to customize the behavior of password management. For example, the "-l" option can be used to lock a user account, preventing the user from logging in until the account is unlocked. To lock the user account "john," users can type "passwd -l john" in the CLI. Similarly, the "-u" option can be used to unlock a previously locked user account. To unlock the user account "john," users can type "passwd -u john" in the CLI. Furthermore, users can use the "usermod" command to modify existing user accounts in the CLI. The "usermod" command allows users to change various attributes of user accounts, such as the username, UID, primary group, home directory, and login shell. For example, to change the login shell for the user account "john" to "/bin/bash," users can type "usermod -s /bin/bash john" in the CLI. Upon executing the command, the "usermod" command will update the login shell for the specified user account accordingly. Moreover, users can use the "deluser" or "userdel" command to delete existing user accounts in the CLI. The "deluser" command is a user-friendly wrapper for the "userdel" command and provides additional options for removing user accounts and their associated files. For example, to delete the user account "john" and remove its home directory and mail spool, users can type "deluser --remove-home --remove-mail john" in the CLI. Alternatively, users can use the "userdel" command to delete user accounts directly from the CLI. For example, to delete the user account "jane" without removing its home directory and mail spool, users can type "userdel jane" in the CLI. In summary, creating and managing user accounts is an essential task for system administrators in Unix-like operating systems. By using commands such as "adduser," "useradd," "passwd," "usermod," "deluser," and "userdel," users can create new user accounts, set passwords, modify account attributes, and delete existing accounts, ensuring efficient user management and system security.

User groups and permissions are essential components of Unix-like operating systems, including Linux, enabling administrators to control access to files and directories effectively. In Unix-based systems, each user account is associated with one or more groups, determining the permissions granted to users for accessing files and directories. The "groups" command can display the groups to which a user belongs. By typing "groups" followed by the username in the CLI, users can see a list of groups to which the specified user belongs. For example, to display the groups associated with the user "john," users can type "groups john" in the CLI. Additionally, users can use the "id" command to view detailed information about a user's identity and group memberships. By typing "id" followed by the username in the CLI, users can see the user ID (UID), group ID (GID), and supplementary group IDs associated with the specified user. For example, to view information about the user "john," users can type "id john" in the CLI. Moreover, user groups are used to manage permissions for files and directories through access control lists (ACLs). ACLs define who can read, write, or execute files and directories, allowing administrators to enforce security policies and restrict access to sensitive information. The "chmod" command is used to modify permissions for files and directories in the CLI. By typing "chmod" followed by the desired permission settings and the target file or directory, users can change permissions accordingly. For example, to grant read and write permissions to the owner of a file named "example.txt," users can type "chmod u+rw example.txt" in the CLI. Similarly, users can use the "chown" command to change the group ownership of files and directories in the CLI. By typing "chown" followed by the new group and the target file or directory, users can transfer ownership accordingly. For example, to change the group ownership of "example.txt" to a group named "developers," users can type "chown :developers example.txt" in the CLI. Additionally, users can use the "chgrp" command to change the group ownership of files and directories directly in the CLI. By typing "chgrp" followed by the new group and the target file or directory, users can change group ownership accordingly. For example, to change the group ownership of "example.txt" to a group named "staff," users can type "chgrp staff example.txt" in the CLI. Furthermore, users can use the "umask" command to set default permissions for newly created files and directories in the CLI. The "umask" command allows users to specify a mask that subtracts permissions from the default permissions applied by the system. For example, to set default permissions for newly created files to read and write for the owner and read-only for the group and others, users can type "umask 022" in the CLI. Similarly, to set default permissions for newly created directories to read, write, and execute for the owner and read and execute for the group and others, users can type "umask 002" in the CLI. Moreover, users can use the "sudo" command to perform administrative tasks, such as modifying permissions and group ownership for system files and directories. The "sudo" command allows users to execute commands with superuser or root privileges, enabling them to perform tasks that require elevated permissions. For example, to change permissions for a system configuration file that requires root privileges, users can type "sudo chmod 644 config.txt" in the CLI. Similarly, users can use "sudo" with "chown" and "chgrp" to change ownership and group membership for system files and directories. In summary, user groups and permissions play a vital role in managing access to files and directories in Unix-like operating systems. By understanding how to use commands such as "groups," "id," "chmod," "chown," "chgrp," "umask," and "sudo," users can effectively control access to their data and enforce security policies within the system.

Chapter 6: Exploring Essential Linux Utilities and Tools

Text editors are essential tools for manipulating and creating text-based files in Unix-like operating systems, offering a range of features and functionalities to suit different user preferences and requirements. Among the most commonly used text editors in Unix-like systems are Vim, Nano, and Emacs, each offering its unique set of advantages and capabilities. Vim, short for Vi Improved, is a highly configurable text editor based on the classic Unix editor Vi. It is known for its modal editing capabilities, which allow users to switch between different modes, such as insert mode, command mode, and visual mode, to perform various editing tasks efficiently. To launch Vim from the command line interface (CLI), users can simply type "vim" followed by the name of the file they wish to edit. For example, to edit a file named "example.txt" using Vim, users can type "vim example.txt" in the CLI. Upon launching Vim, users are presented with a command-line interface where they can begin typing and editing text. Nano, on the other hand, is a simple and user-friendly text editor designed to be easy to use, especially for beginners. It provides a straightforward interface with basic text editing functionalities, making it ideal for quick edits and simple text manipulation tasks. To open a file using Nano in the CLI, users can type "nano" followed by the name of the file they wish to edit. For example, to edit a file named "example.txt" using Nano, users can type "nano example.txt" in the CLI. Upon launching Nano, users are presented with a clean and intuitive text editing interface, with helpful shortcuts and commands displayed at the bottom of the screen. Emacs is a powerful and extensible text editor known for its extensive set of features and customizable behavior. It provides a versatile environment for editing text, with support for syntax highlighting, code folding, and integration with various programming languages and development tools. To start Emacs from the CLI, users can type "emacs" followed by the name of the file they wish to edit. For example, to edit a file named "example.txt" using Emacs, users can type "emacs example.txt" in the CLI. Upon launching Emacs, users are presented with a graphical user interface (GUI) that allows them to navigate, edit, and manage text files efficiently. Each of these text editors has its strengths and weaknesses, making them suitable for different use cases and user preferences. Vim's modal editing capabilities and extensive customization options make it popular among power users and developers who require efficient text editing workflows. Nano's simplicity and ease of use make it an excellent choice for beginners and users who need to perform quick edits without learning complex commands or shortcuts. Emacs's extensive feature set and extensibility make it ideal for users who require advanced text editing capabilities and integration with other tools and languages. Overall, the choice of text editor ultimately depends on the user's specific needs, preferences, and level of expertise, with Vim, Nano, and Emacs each offering a unique set of features and functionalities to cater to different user requirements.

Basic system monitoring and management tools are essential for maintaining the stability, performance, and security of a computer system. These tools provide insights into system resources, processes, and performance metrics, allowing administrators to identify and address issues proactively. One of the fundamental tools for system monitoring is the "top" command, which displays real-time information about system processes, CPU usage, memory usage, and other important metrics. To use the "top" command in the command-line interface (CLI), users simply need to type "top" and press Enter. This command opens an interactive display showing a list of running processes sorted by various criteria such as CPU usage. Users can navigate through the list and take actions like killing processes or adjusting priority. Another useful command-line tool for system monitoring is "htop," which is similar to "top" but offers a more user-friendly and interactive interface with color-coded displays and additional features such as tree-view for processes. To run "htop," users can type "htop" in the CLI and press Enter. This command launches the "htop" application, providing a dynamic and customizable view of system processes and resource usage. Disk usage is another critical aspect of system management, and the "df" command is commonly used to check disk space utilization on Unix-like systems. By typing "df" followed by options such as "-h" for human-readable output and the path to the target file system or directory, users can see a summary of disk space usage. For example, to display disk usage for all mounted file systems in a human-readable format, users can type "df -h" in the CLI. Additionally, the "du" command is used to estimate file and directory space usage recursively. By typing "du" followed by options such as "-h" for human-readable output and the path to the target directory, users can see the disk space usage of files and directories within the specified location. For example, to estimate disk space usage for the "/var/log" directory in a human-readable format, users can type "du -h /var/log" in the CLI. Memory management is crucial for system performance, and the "free" command provides information about available and used memory in the system. By typing "free" followed by options such as "-h" for human-readable output, users can see a summary of memory usage, including total, used, and free memory. For example, to display memory usage in a human-readable format, users can type "free -h" in the CLI. Additionally, the "vmstat" command is used to provide information about virtual memory statistics, including memory, disk, and CPU usage. By typing "vmstat" followed by options such as "-s" for summary output and the refresh interval in seconds, users can see detailed statistics about system memory usage and performance. For example, to display virtual memory statistics in summary format with a refresh interval of 5 seconds, users can type "vmstat -s 5" in the CLI. System logs are valuable sources of information for monitoring system events and diagnosing issues, and the "tail" command is commonly used to view the end of log files in real-time. By typing "tail" followed by options such as "-f" for following the end of the file and the path to the target log file, users can monitor log file updates as they occur. For example, to follow updates to the system log file "/var/log/syslog" in real-time, users can type "tail -f /var/log/syslog" in the CLI. Additionally, the "journalctl" command is used to query and view logs from the systemd journal, a centralized logging system used in many modern Linux distributions. By typing "journalctl" followed by options such as "-f" for following new entries and additional filters for querying specific logs, users can access and analyze journal logs efficiently. For example, to follow new entries in the journal in real-time, users can type "journalctl -f" in the CLI. Security is paramount in system management, and the "iptables" command is commonly used to manage firewall rules on Linux systems. By typing "iptables" followed by options such as "-L" for listing current rules and "-A" for appending new rules, users can configure firewall rules to control incoming and outgoing network traffic. For example, to list current firewall rules, users can type "iptables -L" in the CLI. Similarly, the "ufw" (Uncomplicated Firewall) command provides a simpler interface for managing firewall rules on Linux systems. By typing "ufw" followed by options such as "allow" or "deny" and the port number or service name, users can configure firewall rules quickly and easily. For example, to allow incoming traffic on port 80 (HTTP), users can type "ufw allow 80" in the CLI. In summary, basic system monitoring and management tools are essential for ensuring the stability, performance, and security of computer systems. By using commands such as "top," "htop," "df," "du," "free," "vmstat," "tail," "journalctl," "iptables," and "ufw," administrators can monitor system resources, diagnose issues, and manage system configurations efficiently from the command line interface.

Chapter 7: Networking Essentials in Linux

Configuring network interfaces is a fundamental task in setting up and managing network connectivity on Unix-like operating systems, allowing computers to communicate with other devices and access resources on local and remote networks. The "ifconfig" command, which stands for "interface configuration," is commonly used to view and configure network interfaces in Unix-like systems. By typing "ifconfig" followed by the name of the network interface and options such as IP address, subnet mask, and broadcast address, users can configure network settings for the specified interface. For example, to assign the IP address "192.168.1.100" to the network interface "eth0," users can type "ifconfig eth0 192.168.1.100" in the command-line interface (CLI). Additionally, users can specify options such as "-netmask" and "-broadcast" to set the subnet mask and broadcast address, respectively. For example, to set the subnet mask to "255.255.255.0" and the broadcast address to "192.168.1.255" for the network interface "eth0," users can type "ifconfig eth0 192.168.1.100 netmask 255.255.255.0 broadcast 192.168.1.255" in the CLI. Moreover, the "ip" command, which is part of the iproute2 package, provides a more powerful and flexible alternative to "ifconfig" for configuring network interfaces in modern Linux distributions. By typing "ip addr" followed by options such as "add" to add an IP address to a network interface, users can configure network settings efficiently. For example, to assign the IP address "192.168.1.100" with a subnet mask of "255.255.255.0" to the network interface "eth0," users can type "ip addr add 192.168.1.100/24 dev eth0" in the CLI. Similarly, users can use the "ip link" command to manage network interfaces, including enabling, disabling, and renaming interfaces. For example, to bring up the network interface "eth0," users can type "ip link set eth0 up" in the CLI. Conversely, to bring down the interface, users can type "ip link set eth0 down." Additionally, users can use the "nmcli" command, which is part of the NetworkManager package, to manage network interfaces and connections in Linux distributions that use NetworkManager for network configuration. By typing "nmcli connection show" followed by options such as "up" to bring up a network connection or "down" to bring it down, users can control network interfaces and connections efficiently. For example, to bring up the network connection named "Wired connection 1," users can type "nmcli connection up 'Wired connection 1'" in the CLI. Similarly, to bring down the connection, users can type "nmcli connection down 'Wired connection 1'." Moreover, users can use the "ifup" and "ifdown" commands to bring up or down network interfaces manually. The "ifup" command brings up a network interface specified in the "/etc/network/interfaces" configuration file, while "ifdown" shuts down the interface. For example, to bring up the network interface "eth0" configured in the "/etc/network/interfaces" file, users can type "ifup eth0" in the CLI. Conversely, to bring down the interface, users can type "ifdown eth0." Additionally, users can configure network interfaces permanently by editing the "/etc/network/interfaces" configuration file directly. This file contains network interface configuration settings, including IP addresses, subnet masks, gateway addresses, and DNS servers. By editing this file with a text editor such as "nano" or "vim," users can specify the desired network settings for each interface. For example, to configure the network interface "eth0" with a static IP address, users can open the "/etc/network/interfaces" file in a text editor, add the appropriate configuration lines, and save the changes. In summary, configuring network interfaces is a crucial task in setting up and managing network connectivity on Unix-like operating systems. By using commands such as "ifconfig," "ip," "nmcli," "ifup," and "ifdown," as well as editing configuration files like "/etc/network/interfaces," users can configure network settings efficiently and ensure reliable network connectivity for their systems.

Introduction to network services is essential for understanding how computers communicate and share resources over networks, facilitating various functionalities such as remote access, file transfer, and domain name resolution. Secure Shell (SSH) is a cryptographic network protocol that provides secure communication over unsecured networks, allowing users to access and manage remote systems securely. The "ssh" command is used to establish SSH connections to remote hosts, enabling users to log in remotely and execute commands securely. By typing "ssh" followed by the username and hostname or IP address of the remote system, users can initiate an SSH session. For example, to connect to a remote system with the username "user" and the hostname "example.com," users can type "ssh user@example.com" in the command-line interface (CLI). Additionally, users can specify options such as "-p" to specify a custom SSH port and "-i" to specify a private key file for authentication. For example, to connect to a remote system on port 2222 with a private key file named "id_rsa," users can type "ssh -p 2222 -i ~/.ssh/id_rsa user@example.com" in the CLI. Furthermore, File Transfer Protocol (FTP) is a standard network protocol used for transferring files between a client and a server on a computer network. The "ftp" command is commonly used to interact with FTP servers, enabling users to upload, download, and manage files remotely. By typing "ftp" followed by the hostname or IP address of the FTP server, users can initiate an FTP session. For example, to connect to an FTP server hosted at "ftp.example.com," users can type "ftp ftp.example.com" in the CLI. Once connected, users can use commands such as "get" to download files from the server, "put" to upload files to the server, and "ls" to list files and directories on the server. Additionally, users can use options such as "-u" to specify the username and "-p" to specify the password for authentication. For example, to connect to an FTP server with the username "user" and password "password," users can type "ftp -u user -p password ftp.example.com" in the CLI. Moreover, Domain Name System (DNS) is a hierarchical and decentralized naming system for computers, services, or other resources connected to the internet or a private network. DNS translates domain names into IP addresses, allowing users to access resources using human-readable names instead of numerical IP addresses. The "nslookup" command is commonly used to query DNS servers and retrieve information about domain names, IP addresses, and other DNS records. By typing "nslookup" followed by the domain name or IP address, users can perform DNS lookups and obtain information about the specified resource. For example, to perform a DNS lookup for the domain name "example.com," users can type "nslookup example.com" in the CLI. Additionally, users can specify options such as "-type" to specify the type of DNS record to query, such as "A" for IPv4 addresses, "AAAA" for IPv6 addresses, "MX" for mail exchange records, and "NS" for name server records. For example, to query the mail exchange records for the domain name "example.com," users can type "nslookup -type=MX example.com" in the CLI. Furthermore, users can use the "dig" command, which is another DNS lookup utility, to query DNS servers and retrieve information about domain names and DNS records. By typing "dig" followed by options such as "+short" to display only the IP addresses and the domain name or IP address, users can perform DNS lookups efficiently. For example, to obtain the IPv4 address of the domain name "example.com," users can type "dig +short example.com" in the CLI. Similarly, to obtain the IPv6 address of the domain name "example.com," users can type "dig +short AAAA example.com" in the CLI. In summary, understanding network services such as SSH, FTP, and DNS is essential for managing network connectivity, accessing remote systems, transferring files, and resolving domain names. By using commands such as "ssh," "ftp," "nslookup," and "dig," users can interact with these services effectively and utilize them to accomplish various network-related tasks.

Chapter 8: Becoming a Linux System Administrator: Advanced Techniques

Managing software packages with package managers is a fundamental aspect of maintaining and updating software on Unix-like operating systems, enabling users to install, update, and remove software packages efficiently. Package managers automate the process of software management by handling dependencies, resolving conflicts, and ensuring system integrity. One of the most commonly used package managers in Unix-like systems is Advanced Package Tool (APT), which is used in Debian-based distributions such as Ubuntu. The "apt" command is the primary interface for APT package management, allowing users to perform various package management tasks. To install a package using APT, users can type "sudo apt install" followed by the name of the package in the command-line interface (CLI). For example, to install the "firefox" web browser, users can type "sudo apt install firefox." Additionally, users can use the "update" command to refresh the package lists from the repositories and ensure that the latest versions of packages are available. By typing "sudo apt update" in the CLI, users can update the package lists. Furthermore, users can use the "upgrade" command to upgrade installed packages to their latest versions. By typing "sudo apt upgrade" in the CLI, users can upgrade all installed packages to their latest versions. Additionally, users can use the "remove" command to uninstall packages from the system. By typing "sudo apt remove" followed by the name of the package in the CLI, users can remove the specified package. Moreover, users can use the "autoremove" command to remove packages that were installed as dependencies but are no longer needed by any other packages. By typing "sudo apt autoremove" in the CLI, users can remove orphaned packages. Another widely used package manager in Unix-like systems is YUM (Yellowdog Updater, Modified), which is used in Red Hat-based distributions such as CentOS and Fedora. The "yum" command is the primary interface for YUM package management, allowing users to perform various package management tasks. To install a package using YUM, users can type "sudo yum install" followed by the name of the package in the CLI. For example, to install the "httpd" web server, users can type "sudo yum install httpd." Additionally, users can use the "update" command to update installed packages to their latest versions. By typing "sudo yum update" in the CLI, users can update all installed packages. Furthermore, users can use the "remove" command to uninstall packages from the system. By typing "sudo yum remove" followed by the name of the package in the CLI, users can remove the specified package. Moreover, users can use the "clean" command to remove cached package data from the system. By typing "sudo yum clean all" in the CLI, users can clean the package cache. Another commonly used package manager in Unix-like systems is Pacman, which is used in Arch Linux and its derivatives. The "pacman" command is the primary interface for Pacman package management, allowing users to perform various package management tasks. To install a package using Pacman, users can type "sudo pacman -S" followed by the name of the package in the CLI. For example, to install the "vim" text editor, users can type "sudo pacman -S vim." Additionally, users can use the "-Syu" option to synchronize package databases and upgrade installed packages to their latest versions. By typing "sudo pacman -Syu" in the CLI, users can synchronize package databases and upgrade all installed packages. Furthermore, users can use the "-R" option to remove packages from the system. By typing "sudo pacman -R" followed by the name of the package in the CLI, users can remove the specified package. Moreover, users can use the "-Sc" option to remove cached package data from the system. By typing "sudo pacman -Sc" in the CLI, users can clean the package cache. In summary, managing software packages with package managers is essential for maintaining and updating software on Unix-like operating systems. By using commands such as "apt," "yum," and "pacman," users can install, update, and remove packages efficiently, ensuring system integrity and stability.

Advanced system administration tasks encompass a range of crucial responsibilities including backup, restore, and security measures, each playing a pivotal role in maintaining system integrity and data protection. Backing up data is a fundamental practice in system administration, safeguarding against data loss due to hardware failures, software errors, or malicious attacks. The "tar" command, short for "tape archive," is a versatile tool used to create and manipulate archive files. To create a backup archive of a directory, users can type "tar -cvzf backup.tar.gz /path/to/directory" in the command-line interface (CLI), where "-c" denotes creating an archive, "-v" enables verbose output, "-z" compresses the archive using gzip, and "-f" specifies the filename. Additionally, users can employ tools like "rsync" for efficient file synchronization and backup operations, facilitating incremental backups by transferring only the changed parts of files. By typing "rsync -avz /source/directory/ /destination/directory" in the CLI, users can synchronize the contents of the source directory with the destination directory, preserving permissions, and recursively copying subdirectories. Moreover, leveraging cloud storage services such as Amazon S3, Google Cloud Storage, or Dropbox enables users to store backups offsite, enhancing data redundancy and disaster recovery capabilities. Integrating automated backup solutions like "cron" jobs ensures regular and consistent backup routines, minimizing the risk of data loss. Furthermore, implementing a robust backup rotation strategy, such as the Grandfather-Father-Son (GFS) method, allows for efficient management of backup archives over time, balancing storage requirements and data retention periods. In the event of data loss or system failure, the ability to restore data swiftly is paramount. Utilizing backup tools like "tar" or "rsync," users can extract files from backup archives by typing commands such as "tar -xvzf backup.tar.gz" or "rsync -avz /backup/directory/ /restore/directory" in the CLI, restoring data to its original location or an alternative destination. Additionally, employing version control systems such as Git enables users to track changes to files and revert to previous states, facilitating granular data restoration and version management. Implementing disk imaging solutions like "Clonezilla" or "dd" allows users to create exact replicas of entire disk partitions or drives, enabling comprehensive system recovery in the event of catastrophic failures. Furthermore, leveraging virtualization technologies such as VMware vSphere or Microsoft Hyper-V facilitates rapid deployment of virtual machine snapshots, providing instantaneous recovery points for critical systems. Security is a paramount concern in system administration, encompassing a multitude of measures aimed at protecting systems, networks, and data from unauthorized access, breaches, or exploitation. Employing strong authentication mechanisms such as Secure Shell (SSH) keys or multi-factor authentication (MFA) enhances access control and mitigates the risk of unauthorized access to systems. By generating SSH key pairs using commands like "ssh-keygen" and configuring SSH servers to use key-based authentication, users can establish secure, password-less access to remote systems. Implementing access control mechanisms such as file permissions, Access Control Lists (ACLs), and

Role-Based Access Control (RBAC) enables users to restrict access to sensitive resources and enforce least privilege principles, reducing the attack surface and limiting the impact of security incidents. Additionally, deploying intrusion detection and prevention systems (IDS/IPS) like Snort or Suricata enables real-time monitoring of network traffic, detecting and mitigating suspicious activities or malicious behavior. Moreover, implementing robust firewall rules using tools like iptables or firewalld helps filter incoming and outgoing network traffic, enforcing security policies and protecting against network-based attacks. Regularly updating and patching systems and software is critical to addressing known vulnerabilities and mitigating security risks. By executing commands like "apt update && apt upgrade" or "yum update" in the CLI, users can update system packages and apply security patches to mitigate potential vulnerabilities. Furthermore, conducting regular security audits and vulnerability assessments helps identify and remediate security weaknesses, ensuring continuous improvement of security posture. Emphasizing security awareness and training for system administrators and end-users is essential in fostering a security-conscious culture, promoting adherence to security best practices, and mitigating the risk of social engineering attacks or human errors. Implementing data encryption mechanisms such as full disk encryption (FDE), encrypted filesystems, or Transport Layer Security (TLS) encryption for network communications safeguards sensitive data against unauthorized access or interception. Additionally, leveraging security information and event management (SIEM) solutions like Splunk or ELK Stack enables centralized log aggregation, analysis, and correlation, facilitating proactive threat detection and incident response. Implementing robust backup, restore, and security measures is paramount in advanced system administration, safeguarding against data loss, system failures, and security breaches. By leveraging backup tools, disk imaging solutions, and version control systems, users can ensure data integrity and facilitate rapid recovery in the event of disasters. Furthermore, implementing stringent access controls, security mechanisms, and regular security updates strengthens the overall security posture and mitigates the risk of unauthorized access or exploitation.

BOOK 3

UNLOCKING UNIX

ADVANCED TECHNIQUES FOR OPERATING SYSTEM VETERANS

ROB BOTWRIGHT

Chapter 1: Advanced Shell Scripting and Automation

Scripting fundamentals are essential for automating tasks and streamlining workflows in Unix-like operating systems, enabling users to write scripts that execute a series of commands automatically. At the core of scripting are variables, which are used to store data and values for later use. In Bash scripting, variables are declared by assigning a value to a name. For example, to declare a variable named "name" with the value "John," users can type "name=John" in the command-line interface (CLI). Additionally, users can use variables to store command output and use it later in the script. For example, to store the output of the "date" command in a variable named "current_date," users can type "current_date=$(date)" in the CLI. Furthermore, scripting often involves using loops to iterate over a series of items or perform a set of actions repeatedly. One common type of loop is the "for" loop, which iterates over a list of items. For example, to iterate over a list of filenames in a directory and print each filename, users can use the following Bash script:

bashCopy code

```
for file in *; do echo "$file" done
```

In this script, the "for" loop iterates over each filename in the current directory, and the "echo" command prints each filename to the standard output. Moreover, users can use conditionals to execute different commands based on specified conditions. One common type of conditional is the "if" statement, which evaluates a condition and executes a block of code if the condition is true. For example, to check if a file named "example.txt" exists in the current directory and print a message if it does, users can use the following Bash script:

bashCopy code

```
if [ -e "example.txt" ]; then echo "File exists." fi
```

In this script, the "-e" flag checks if the file "example.txt" exists, and if it does, the "echo" command prints the message "File exists." Additionally, users can use logical operators such as "&&" for "and" and "||" for "or" to combine multiple conditions in a single statement. For example, to check if both files "file1.txt" and "file2.txt" exist in the current directory and print a message if they do, users can use the following Bash script:

bashCopy code

if [-e "file1.txt"] && [-e "file2.txt"]; then echo "Both files exist." fi

In this script, the "&&" operator combines two conditions, and the "echo" command prints the message "Both files exist" if both conditions are true. Moreover, users can use control structures such as "while" loops and "case" statements to implement more complex logic in scripts. For example, the "while" loop executes a block of code repeatedly as long as a specified condition is true, while the "case" statement evaluates a value against multiple possible patterns and executes the corresponding block of code for the first matching pattern. In summary, scripting fundamentals such as variables, loops, and conditionals are essential for automating tasks and writing efficient scripts in Unix-like operating systems. By mastering these fundamentals and understanding how to use them effectively, users can create powerful scripts that automate repetitive tasks and improve productivity.

Automation techniques play a pivotal role in streamlining tasks and optimizing workflows in Unix-like operating systems, enhancing efficiency and productivity. One of the fundamental automation techniques is the use of cron jobs, which allow users to schedule repetitive tasks to run automatically at specified intervals. The "crontab" command is used to create, modify, and view cron jobs in Unix-like systems. By typing "crontab -e" in the command-line interface (CLI), users can edit their cron jobs using the default text editor specified in the system's environment variables. Within the crontab file, users can define cron jobs using the cron syntax, specifying the schedule and command to be executed. For example, to schedule a script named "backup.sh" to run every day at 2:00 AM, users can add the following line to their crontab file: "0 2 * * * /path/to/backup.sh." This cron job will execute the "backup.sh" script daily at 2:00 AM. Additionally, users can use the "crontab -l" command to list their current cron jobs, allowing them to review and verify their scheduled tasks. Moreover, shell functions are another powerful automation technique that allows users to define reusable code blocks within shell scripts. Shell functions encapsulate a sequence of commands or operations into a single named entity, providing modularity and maintainability to shell scripts. To define a shell function, users can use the following syntax in their shell scripts: "function_name() { commands }." For example, to create a function named "backup_data" that archives files from a specified directory, users can define the function as follows:

bashCopy code

```
backup_data() { tar -czf /path/to/backup.tar.gz /path/to/files }
```

This shell function uses the "tar" command to create a compressed archive of files from the specified directory. Once defined, users can invoke the shell function within their shell scripts by simply calling its name. For example, to execute the "backup_data" function, users can add the following line to their shell script:

bashCopy code

```
backup_data
```

This line will execute the "backup_data" function, creating a backup archive of files as defined within the function. Furthermore, users can pass arguments to shell functions to customize their behavior based on runtime parameters. Shell functions support positional parameters, allowing users to access arguments passed to the function within its body. For example, to modify the "backup_data" function to accept a directory path as an argument, users can define the function as follows:

bashCopy code

```
backup_data() { directory=$1 tar -czf /path/to/backup.tar.gz "$directory" }
```

In this modified version of the function, the directory path is assigned to the "directory" variable, which is then used as an argument to the "tar" command. Users can then invoke the function with the desired directory path as an argument, allowing for greater flexibility and reusability. In summary, automation techniques such as cron jobs and shell functions are indispensable tools for automating repetitive tasks and improving productivity in Unix-like operating systems. By leveraging cron jobs, users can schedule tasks to run automatically at specified intervals, while shell functions provide modularity and reusability to shell scripts, enabling users to encapsulate complex operations into reusable components. Through the effective use of these automation techniques, users can streamline their workflows, enhance system efficiency, and focus on higher-level tasks.

Chapter 2: Mastering System Processes and Management

Understanding processes and process management commands is essential for efficient system administration and troubleshooting in Unix-like operating systems. Processes are running instances of programs or tasks within the operating system, each with its unique process ID (PID), state, and associated system resources. The "ps" command is one of the fundamental tools for listing processes in Unix-like systems, allowing users to view information about running processes. By typing "ps" in the command-line interface (CLI), users can display a snapshot of active processes on the system. Additionally, users can specify options such as "-aux" to display detailed information about all processes, including those owned by other users, and "-ef" to display a full listing of processes with additional information such as parent process IDs (PPIDs). For example, to list all processes on the system along with detailed information, users can type "ps -aux" in the CLI. Moreover, users can use the "top" command to dynamically monitor system processes and resource usage in real-time. By typing "top" in the CLI, users can display an interactive table showing processes sorted by various criteria such as CPU and memory usage. Additionally, users can use options such as "-o" to specify the sorting order and "-n" to set the number of iterations. For example, to display the top processes consuming the most CPU resources, users can type "top -o %CPU" in the CLI. Furthermore, users can use the "htop" command, which is an enhanced version of "top," to interactively monitor and manage system processes. By typing "htop" in the CLI, users can display an interactive process viewer with color-coded metrics and keyboard shortcuts for managing processes. Additionally, users can use options such as "-u" to filter processes by user and "-p" to specify the process ID to monitor. For example, to display processes owned by the user "user1" using htop, users can type "htop -u user1" in the CLI. Moreover, users can use the "kill" command to terminate processes based on their process IDs. By typing "kill" followed by the PID of the process to be terminated, users can send a termination signal to the specified process. Additionally, users can use options such as "-9" to send a forceful termination signal (SIGKILL) to the process. For example, to terminate a process with PID 1234, users can type "kill 1234" in the CLI.

Furthermore, users can use the "killall" command to terminate processes based on their names. By typing "killall" followed by the name of the process to be terminated, users can send termination signals to all processes with matching names. Additionally, users can use options such as "-r" to interpret the process name as a regular expression and "-e" to specify the exact match. For example, to terminate all instances of the process "firefox," users can type "killall firefox" in the CLI. In summary, understanding processes and process management commands is crucial for system administration and troubleshooting in Unix-like operating systems. By using commands such as "ps," "top," "htop," "kill," and "killall," users can monitor, manage, and terminate processes effectively, ensuring system stability and performance.

Advanced process monitoring and control techniques are essential for system administrators to effectively manage system resources, troubleshoot performance issues, and ensure optimal system operation. While basic process monitoring commands like "ps" and "top" provide valuable insights into running processes, advanced techniques offer more granular control and visibility. One such technique is process prioritization using the "nice" and "renice" commands. The "nice" command allows users to adjust the priority of a process at launch, with lower values indicating higher priority. For instance, to start a process with a lower priority, users can precede the command with "nice -n [value]." Conversely, the "renice" command alters the priority of an existing process, requiring the process ID (PID) as an argument. For example, to increase the priority of a process with PID 1234, users can issue the command "renice -n [-value] 1234" in the CLI. Additionally, users can employ process grouping and management techniques using tools like "pgrep," "pkill," and "psgrep." These commands allow users to search for and manipulate groups of processes based on various criteria such as name, user, and memory usage. For instance, to list processes with a specific name, users can employ "pgrep [name]." Similarly, "pkill [name]" terminates processes based on their name, offering a convenient alternative to manually identifying and terminating processes. Furthermore, users can utilize process monitoring utilities like "htop" and "atop" for real-time process visualization and resource tracking. "htop" provides an interactive interface displaying process metrics such as CPU and memory usage, facilitating efficient process management. On the other hand, "atop" offers advanced system-wide performance monitoring, allowing users to analyze historical data and identify resource bottlenecks. Additionally, system administrators can implement process accounting to track resource consumption and user activity over time. By enabling process accounting with commands like "accton" and "sa," administrators can generate reports detailing process usage, facilitating resource optimization and accountability. Moreover, users can employ process tracing tools like "strace" and "ltrace" to monitor system calls and library functions invoked by processes. These utilities aid in debugging and performance tuning by providing insight into process behavior and dependencies. For example, "strace [command]" traces system calls made by a process, enabling users to identify errors and inefficiencies in program execution. Similarly, "ltrace [command]" tracks library calls, revealing dependencies and performance bottlenecks associated with shared libraries. Additionally, users can leverage kernel-level tracing frameworks like "eBPF" (extended Berkeley Packet Filter) for advanced process monitoring and analysis. eBPF allows users to attach lightweight programs to kernel events, enabling custom instrumentation and monitoring of process behavior. By deploying eBPF scripts with tools like "bpftrace" and "bpftool," administrators can gain deep insights into process interactions and system performance. Furthermore, users can implement process supervision and fault tolerance mechanisms using tools like "systemd" and "supervisord." These utilities facilitate automated process management, ensuring continuous availability and resilience against failures. For example, "systemd" enables users to define and manage system services, providing features like service dependencies, automatic restarts, and resource limits. Similarly, "supervisord" offers process supervision capabilities, allowing users to monitor and control application processes within a managed environment. In summary, mastering advanced process monitoring and control techniques is crucial for system administrators to maintain system stability, optimize resource utilization, and troubleshoot performance issues effectively. By leveraging commands, utilities, and frameworks discussed above, administrators can gain deeper insights into process behavior, implement proactive monitoring solutions, and ensure reliable operation of Unix-like systems.

Chapter 3: Advanced File System Administration

File system management tools and utilities are indispensable for maintaining, organizing, and optimizing file systems in Unix-like operating systems. These tools offer a range of functionalities, from basic file manipulation to advanced disk partitioning and filesystem integrity checks. One of the most commonly used tools for file system management is "ls," which lists directory contents. By typing "ls" in the command-line interface (CLI), users can display the files and directories within the current directory. Additionally, users can utilize options such as "-l" to list files in long format, providing detailed information like file permissions, ownership, size, and modification date. Furthermore, "ls" can be combined with other commands like "grep" to filter directory contents based on specific criteria. For instance, to list only files with a particular extension, users can pipe the output of "ls" to "grep" using the command "ls | grep '.txt'." Another essential tool for file system management is "cp," which copies files and directories. By typing "cp [source] [destination]" in the CLI, users can copy files from a source location to a destination location. Moreover, users can use options such as "-r" to copy directories recursively and "-v" to display verbose output. For example, to copy a directory named "docs" and its contents to another location, users can type "cp -r docs /destination/path" in the CLI. Additionally, users can employ the "mv" command to move or rename files and directories. By typing "mv [source] [destination]" in the CLI, users can move files from one location to another or rename them. Similarly to "cp," "mv" supports options like "-v" for verbose output and "-i" to prompt for confirmation before overwriting existing files. For instance, to move a file named "file1" to a directory named "folder," users can type "mv file1 folder" in the CLI. Moreover, users can utilize the "rm" command to remove files and directories. By typing "rm [file]" or "rm -r [directory]" in the CLI, users can delete files or directories, respectively. Additionally, users can use options like "-f" to force deletion without prompting for confirmation and "-i" to prompt for confirmation before each removal. For example, to delete a file named "file1," users can type "rm file1" in the CLI. Furthermore, users can employ file compression tools like "gzip" and "bzip2" to reduce file sizes and save disk space. These utilities allow users to compress files into gzip or bzip2 formats using commands like "gzip [file]" and "bzip2 [file]." Additionally, users can use options like "-d" to decompress compressed files. For example, to compress a file named "file1," users can type "gzip file1" in the CLI. Similarly, to decompress a file named "file1.gz," users can type "gzip -d file1.gz." In addition to basic file manipulation, file system management tools include utilities for disk partitioning, formatting, and filesystem integrity checks. One such utility is "fdisk," which is used for disk partitioning. By typing "fdisk [device]" in the CLI, users can create, delete, and modify disk partitions. Additionally, users can use options like "-l" to list existing partitions and "-n" to create a new partition. For example, to create a new partition on the disk "sdb," users can type "fdisk /dev/sdb" in the CLI. Furthermore, users can utilize the "mkfs" command to format partitions with a specific filesystem. By typing "mkfs -t [filesystem] [device]" in the CLI, users can format partitions with filesystems like ext4, xfs, or ntfs. Moreover, users can employ filesystem integrity check tools like "fsck" to repair corrupted filesystems. By typing "fsck [device]" in the CLI, users can scan and repair filesystem errors on a specified device. Additionally, users can use options like "-f" to force a filesystem check and "-y" to automatically repair filesystem errors without prompting for confirmation. For example, to check and repair the filesystem on the partition "sdb1," users can type "fsck /dev/sdb1" in the CLI. In summary, file system management tools and utilities are essential for managing, organizing, and optimizing file systems in Unix-like operating systems. By utilizing commands like "ls," "cp," "mv," "rm," and utilities like "fdisk," "mkfs," and "fsck," users can perform a wide range of file system management tasks efficiently and effectively, ensuring the integrity and reliability of their storage infrastructure.

File system optimization and maintenance are critical tasks for ensuring the efficient operation and longevity of storage systems in Unix-like operating environments. These tasks encompass a range of techniques aimed at enhancing file system performance, preventing data loss, and prolonging the lifespan of storage devices. One fundamental aspect of file system optimization is periodic disk defragmentation, particularly relevant for traditional spinning hard disk drives (HDDs). Fragmentation occurs when files are stored in non-contiguous clusters on the disk, leading to increased seek times and reduced read/write performance. The "fsck" command is commonly used to check and repair filesystem inconsistencies in Unix-like systems. By typing "fsck [device]" in the CLI, users can scan the filesystem for errors and automatically repair them. Additionally, users can use options like "-f" to force a filesystem check and "-y" to automatically repair filesystem errors without prompting for confirmation. For example, to check and repair the filesystem on the partition "sdb1," users can type "fsck /dev/sdb1" in the CLI. Another vital aspect of file system maintenance is ensuring adequate disk space availability and preventing filesystems from becoming full, which can lead to performance degradation and system instability. The "df" command is a valuable tool for monitoring disk space usage in Unix-like systems. By typing "df -h" in the CLI, users can display disk space usage information in a human-readable format, including total, used, and available space for each mounted filesystem. Moreover, users can use the "du" command to determine disk space usage by specific directories and files. By typing "du -h [directory]" in the CLI, users can display disk space usage information for the specified directory and its subdirectories in a human-readable format. Additionally, users can use options like "-s" to display summarized disk space usage and "-h" to show sizes in a human-readable format. For example, to display disk space usage for the "/home" directory, users can type "du -h /home" in the CLI. File system optimization also involves optimizing file access patterns and improving read/write performance through techniques such as caching and prefetching. The "sync" command is frequently used to flush file system buffers to disk, ensuring data integrity and preventing data loss in the event of a system crash or power failure. By typing "sync" in the CLI, users can synchronize cached data with disk storage, minimizing the risk of data corruption. Additionally, users can employ the "fstrim" command to discard unused data blocks on SSDs, enhancing write performance and extending SSD lifespan. By typing "fstrim [mountpoint]" in the CLI, users can trim unused blocks on the specified filesystem, freeing up space and improving write performance. Moreover, users can use options like "-v" to display verbose output and "-a" to trim all mounted filesystems. For example, to trim unused blocks on the "/home" filesystem, users can type "fstrim /home" in the CLI. Regular backup and data archiving are essential components of file system maintenance, enabling users to recover lost or corrupted data in the event of hardware failure, malware attacks, or accidental deletion. The "tar" command is a versatile tool for creating and managing compressed archive files in Unix-like systems. By typing "tar -cvzf [archive_name.tar.gz] [source_directory]" in the CLI, users can create a compressed archive of the specified directory and its contents. Additionally, users can use options like "-c" to create a new archive, "-v" for verbose output, "-z" to compress the archive using gzip, and "-f" to specify the archive filename. For example, to create a compressed archive of the "/home/user" directory named "backup.tar.gz," users can type "tar -cvzf backup.tar.gz /home/user" in the CLI. Furthermore, users can employ the "rsync" command for efficient file synchronization and remote backups. By typing "rsync -av [source_directory] [destination_directory]" in the CLI, users can synchronize the contents of the source directory with the destination directory, ensuring data consistency and integrity. Additionally, users can use options like "-a" for archive mode, preserving file permissions and timestamps, and "-v" for verbose output. For example, to synchronize the "/home/user" directory with a remote server named "backup_server," users can type "rsync -av /home/user backup_server:/backup" in the CLI. In summary, file system optimization and maintenance are essential for ensuring the reliability, performance, and longevity of storage systems in Unix-like operating environments. By implementing techniques such as disk defragmentation, disk space management, data caching, and backup strategies, users can mitigate the risk of data loss, improve system performance, and prolong the lifespan of storage devices.

Chapter 4: Network Configuration and Administration

Advanced networking concepts such as VLANs, routing, and firewalls are integral components of modern network infrastructure, essential for ensuring efficient communication, network segmentation, and security. VLANs, or Virtual Local Area Networks, enable network administrators to logically segment a single physical network into multiple virtual networks, each operating independently. The "vlan" command in Cisco IOS or similar networking devices allows administrators to create, configure, and manage VLANs. For instance, to create a VLAN with ID 10, administrators can access the configuration mode and type "vlan 10" followed by the "name" command to assign a name to the VLAN. Moreover, VLAN trunking protocols like IEEE 802.1Q facilitate the transmission of VLAN traffic across network switches, enabling devices in different VLANs to communicate efficiently. By configuring trunk ports using commands like "switchport mode trunk" and "switchport trunk allowed vlan," administrators can define which VLANs are allowed to traverse trunk links. Additionally, routing plays a crucial role in directing traffic between different networks or subnets, ensuring that data reaches its intended destination. Routing protocols such as OSPF (Open Shortest Path First) and BGP (Border Gateway Protocol) enable routers to exchange routing information and dynamically adjust network routes based on factors like network topology and link availability. In Cisco IOS, administrators can configure OSPF using commands like "router ospf [process-id]" and specify the networks to be advertised using the "network" command under OSPF configuration mode. Similarly, BGP configuration involves commands like "router bgp [autonomous-system]" and the advertisement of network prefixes using the "network" command under BGP configuration mode. Moreover, firewalls serve as a critical line of defense against unauthorized access and malicious threats by filtering incoming and outgoing network traffic based on predefined security rules. Advanced firewall techniques include stateful packet inspection, application-layer filtering, and intrusion prevention systems (IPS). In Cisco ASA (Adaptive Security Appliance) devices, administrators can configure firewall rules using the "access-list" command to define traffic filtering criteria based on source and destination addresses, ports, and protocols. Additionally, advanced features like Cisco Firepower Threat Defense (FTD) provide comprehensive threat detection and mitigation capabilities, leveraging technologies such as Snort-based intrusion detection and Cisco Talos threat intelligence integration. Furthermore, network security policies can be enforced using access control lists (ACLs) to permit or deny traffic based on specific criteria. In Cisco IOS, administrators can create ACLs using commands like "access-list" followed by a numeric or named identifier, specifying permit or deny statements for various traffic types. For example, to create an ACL permitting HTTP traffic from a specific subnet, administrators can type "access-list 101 permit tcp [source] [source-wildcard] [destination] [destination-wildcard] eq www" in global configuration mode. In summary, mastering advanced networking concepts such as VLANs, routing, and firewalls is essential for network administrators to design, deploy, and maintain robust and secure network infrastructures. By leveraging CLI commands and configuration techniques specific to networking devices, administrators can implement efficient VLAN segmentation, dynamic routing protocols, and comprehensive firewall policies, ensuring optimal network performance and security posture.

Network service configuration and optimization are vital aspects of managing a network infrastructure, ensuring efficient communication and reliable service delivery. One fundamental aspect of network service configuration is the setup and optimization of DHCP (Dynamic Host Configuration Protocol) servers, which automate the assignment of IP addresses and network configuration parameters to client devices. In Linux-based systems, administrators can configure the DHCP server using software like ISC DHCP server or Dnsmasq. Using ISC DHCP server, for instance, administrators can edit the "dhcpd.conf" configuration file to define IP address ranges, subnet masks, default gateway, DNS server addresses, and lease durations. They can then start the DHCP server daemon using the command "sudo systemctl start isc-dhcp-server" and enable it to start at boot using "sudo systemctl enable isc-dhcp-server". Additionally, administrators can fine-tune DHCP server performance and scalability by adjusting parameters like subnet sizing and lease duration based on network requirements and client population. Furthermore, optimizing DNS (Domain Name System) resolution is crucial for efficient name resolution and network performance. Administrators can configure DNS servers to improve query response times, reduce latency, and enhance fault tolerance. In Linux systems, administrators can edit the "/etc/resolv.conf" file to specify DNS server IP addresses and domain search suffixes. They can also configure DNS caching servers like BIND or Unbound to cache frequently accessed DNS records, reducing the load on upstream DNS servers and improving response times for subsequent queries. Moreover, administrators can deploy DNSSEC (Domain Name System Security Extensions) to authenticate DNS responses and prevent DNS spoofing attacks, thereby enhancing the security and integrity of DNS resolution. Another aspect of network service configuration and optimization involves configuring and optimizing network file-sharing services such as Samba or NFS (Network File System). These services enable file sharing between heterogeneous systems, facilitating collaborative work environments and centralized data storage. In Linux environments, administrators can configure Samba for Windows file sharing by editing the "smb.conf" configuration file to define shared directories, access permissions, and user authentication settings. They can then start the Samba service using "sudo systemctl start smbd" and enable it to start at boot using "sudo systemctl enable smbd".

Additionally, administrators can optimize file-sharing performance by fine-tuning Samba settings such as buffer sizes, socket options, and asynchronous I/O parameters based on network bandwidth and file transfer requirements. Furthermore, optimizing network service security is essential to protect sensitive data and prevent unauthorized access. Administrators can enhance service security by implementing encryption protocols like TLS/SSL (Transport Layer Security/Secure Sockets Layer) to secure data in transit between clients and servers. For example, administrators can configure the Apache HTTP server to use TLS/SSL encryption by generating SSL certificates and configuring the server to use them for secure communication. They can then enable SSL/TLS support in the server configuration and specify SSL certificate and key file paths. Additionally, administrators can enforce access controls and authentication mechanisms to restrict access to network services based on user credentials, IP addresses, or other criteria. For instance, administrators can configure Apache HTTP server access control using "htpasswd" to create password-protected directories and "Allow" and "Deny" directives to define access rules based on client IP addresses or hostnames. Moreover, administrators can deploy intrusion detection and prevention systems (IDS/IPS) to monitor network traffic for suspicious activities and enforce security policies to mitigate potential threats. IDS/IPS solutions like Snort or Suricata can analyze network packets in real-time, detect known attack signatures, and trigger alerts or block malicious traffic based on predefined rulesets. Additionally, administrators can configure firewall rules to filter incoming and outgoing traffic based on port numbers, IP addresses, or protocol types, enhancing network service security and resilience against cyber threats. In summary, network service configuration and optimization are critical tasks for network administrators to ensure the efficient operation, performance, and security of network services. By deploying DHCP servers, optimizing DNS resolution, configuring file-sharing services, and enhancing service security measures, administrators can create a robust and reliable network infrastructure that meets the needs of modern organizations.

Chapter 5: Security Hardening and Intrusion Detection

Security principles and best practices are essential components of any robust cybersecurity strategy, aimed at safeguarding systems, networks, and data from unauthorized access, breaches, and malicious activities. One fundamental aspect of security is implementing strong access controls to restrict access to sensitive resources and mitigate the risk of unauthorized access. Administrators can enforce access controls using techniques such as role-based access control (RBAC), which assigns permissions to users based on their roles within an organization. In Unix-like operating systems, administrators can manage file and directory permissions using the "chmod" command to set permissions for owner, group, and others. For example, to restrict access to a file named "example.txt" to the file owner only, administrators can use the command "chmod 700 example.txt". Additionally, administrators can implement multi-factor authentication (MFA) to enhance access security by requiring users to provide multiple forms of authentication, such as passwords and one-time codes, before accessing sensitive resources. MFA solutions like Google Authenticator or Duo Security can be integrated with authentication systems to strengthen access controls and prevent unauthorized access. Furthermore, encryption plays a crucial role in protecting data confidentiality and integrity, especially during transmission and storage. Administrators can deploy encryption techniques such as SSL/TLS (Secure Sockets Layer/Transport Layer Security) for encrypting data in transit over networks. In web servers like Apache HTTP Server, administrators can enable SSL/TLS encryption by generating SSL certificates and configuring the server to use them for secure communication. They can then configure SSL/TLS settings in the server configuration file to specify encryption protocols, cipher suites, and certificate paths. Moreover, administrators can implement disk encryption solutions like BitLocker (Windows) or dm-crypt (Linux) to encrypt data at rest on storage devices. By encrypting sensitive data on disks, administrators can prevent unauthorized access to data in case of theft or physical compromise of storage devices. Additionally, network segmentation is a crucial security measure for isolating network resources and limiting the spread of security incidents. Administrators can segment networks into separate subnets or VLANs (Virtual Local Area Networks) based on security requirements and resource dependencies. Using VLANs, administrators can logically partition a single physical network into multiple virtual networks, each with its own set of security policies and access controls. They can configure VLANs on network switches using commands like "vlan" in Cisco IOS or similar networking devices. For example, to create a VLAN with ID 10, administrators can access the configuration mode and type "vlan 10" followed by the "name" command to assign a name to the VLAN. Additionally, administrators can deploy firewalls and intrusion detection/prevention systems (IDS/IPS) to monitor and control traffic between network segments, enforcing security policies and detecting/preventing malicious activities. Firewalls like iptables (Linux) or Windows Firewall (Windows) can be configured to filter incoming and outgoing traffic based on predefined rulesets, while IDS/IPS solutions like Snort or Suricata can analyze network packets in real-time, detect known attack signatures, and trigger alerts or block malicious traffic. Furthermore, regular security audits and vulnerability assessments are essential for identifying and addressing security weaknesses and vulnerabilities within an organization's IT infrastructure. Administrators can conduct security audits using tools like Nessus or OpenVAS to scan systems and networks for known vulnerabilities, misconfigurations, and security flaws. They can then prioritize and remediate identified vulnerabilities to reduce the organization's exposure to potential cyber threats.

Additionally, administrators can implement security policies and procedures to enforce security standards, educate users about security best practices, and ensure compliance with regulatory requirements. Security policies should cover areas such as password management, data encryption, access controls, incident response, and security awareness training. By establishing clear security policies and procedures, organizations can create a security-conscious culture and mitigate the risk of security breaches and data breaches. In summary, security principles and best practices are essential for protecting systems, networks, and data from cyber threats and unauthorized access. By implementing strong access controls, encryption techniques, network segmentation, firewalls, intrusion detection/prevention systems, regular security audits, and security policies, organizations can strengthen their security posture and reduce the risk of security incidents. Intrusion Detection Systems (IDS) and log analysis are integral components of cybersecurity strategies, providing organizations with the capability to detect and respond to security incidents effectively. IDS play a crucial role in monitoring network traffic and system activities for signs of unauthorized access, malicious activities, and security breaches. One commonly used type of IDS is network-based IDS (NIDS), which monitors network traffic in real-time to detect suspicious patterns or anomalies. Administrators can deploy NIDS solutions like Snort or Suricata to analyze network packets and identify known attack signatures or abnormal behavior. Using Snort, for example, administrators can create custom intrusion detection rules to match specific network traffic patterns indicative of malicious activities. They can define rules using Snort's rule syntax and deploy them to the Snort engine for real-time packet analysis. Additionally, host-based IDS (HIDS) monitors activities on individual systems or hosts to detect unauthorized access, file modifications, or other suspicious behavior. HIDS solutions like OSSEC or Tripwire can monitor system logs, file integrity, and registry changes to identify security incidents and raise alerts. Administrators can configure OSSEC to monitor system logs for specific events using its configuration file and define rules for alerting on suspicious activities. Moreover, log analysis is a critical component of intrusion detection and incident response, enabling organizations to review and analyze log data from various sources to identify security incidents and investigate their root causes. Administrators can collect and centralize log data using tools like syslog-ng or ELK (Elasticsearch, Logstash, Kibana) stack for comprehensive log management and analysis. Using syslog-ng, administrators can configure syslog-ng to collect logs from network devices, servers, and applications and forward them to a central log server for storage and analysis. They can then use ELK stack components like Elasticsearch for log storage and indexing, Logstash for log parsing and enrichment, and Kibana for log visualization and analysis. Furthermore, administrators can implement log correlation and analysis techniques to identify patterns or trends indicative of security incidents or attacks. By correlating log data from multiple sources, such as firewall logs, authentication logs, and intrusion detection logs, administrators can gain insights into the scope and impact of security incidents and take appropriate remediation actions. Additionally, administrators can leverage threat intelligence feeds and indicators of compromise (IOCs) to enhance log analysis and detection capabilities. Threat intelligence feeds provide information about known malicious activities, attack signatures, and indicators of compromise that can be used to identify and block malicious traffic or activities. Administrators can integrate threat intelligence feeds into their IDS and log analysis tools to enhance their ability to detect and respond to security threats effectively. Moreover, administrators can automate log analysis and incident response processes using security orchestration, automation, and response (SOAR) platforms. SOAR platforms like Splunk Phantom or

IBM Resilient enable organizations to streamline incident response workflows, automate repetitive tasks, and orchestrate response actions across security tools and systems. By integrating SOAR platforms with IDS, log analysis, and other security tools, organizations can improve their incident detection and response capabilities and reduce the time to detect and mitigate security incidents. In summary, Intrusion Detection Systems and log analysis are critical components of cybersecurity defenses, providing organizations with the capability to detect and respond to security threats effectively. By deploying NIDS and HIDS solutions, centralizing and analyzing log data, correlating log events, leveraging threat intelligence feeds, and automating incident response processes, organizations can strengthen their security posture and reduce the risk of security breaches and data loss.

Chapter 6: Performance Tuning and Optimization

Performance monitoring tools and techniques are essential for ensuring the efficient operation and optimization of IT systems and infrastructure. These tools enable organizations to monitor system resources, identify performance bottlenecks, and optimize resource utilization to deliver optimal performance and user experience. One commonly used performance monitoring tool in Linux environments is "top", which provides real-time insights into system resource usage, including CPU, memory, and disk utilization. Administrators can run the "top" command in the terminal to display a dynamic view of system processes sorted by resource consumption. They can analyze the output to identify processes consuming excessive CPU or memory resources and take appropriate actions to optimize resource usage. Additionally, administrators can use the "ps" command to list running processes and their resource usage statistics. By running "ps aux" or "ps -ef" commands, administrators can display detailed information about all running processes, including their process IDs (PIDs), CPU and memory usage, and execution status. They can then analyze the output to identify processes consuming high CPU or memory resources and investigate further to determine the root cause of performance issues. Moreover, administrators can use performance monitoring tools like "vmstat" to collect and display system-wide performance statistics, including CPU, memory, disk, and network utilization. By running the "vmstat" command with appropriate options, administrators can display real-time and historical performance metrics, such as CPU idle time, memory usage, disk I/O operations, and network traffic. They can use the output to identify performance bottlenecks and optimize system configuration and resource allocation accordingly. Furthermore, administrators can leverage system monitoring frameworks like Nagios or Zabbix to monitor and manage the performance of multiple systems and services from a centralized dashboard. These frameworks provide features for monitoring system metrics, generating alerts on performance issues, and automating response actions. By deploying Nagios or Zabbix agents on target systems and configuring monitoring templates and thresholds, administrators can gain visibility into system performance and proactively address potential issues before they impact users or applications. Additionally, administrators can use benchmarking tools like "sysbench" or "iperf" to assess system performance and measure the impact of configuration changes or optimizations. For example, administrators can use "sysbench" to stress test CPU, memory, or disk subsystems and evaluate system performance under different workload scenarios. They can run "sysbench" commands with appropriate options to execute benchmark tests and analyze the results to identify performance bottlenecks and areas for improvement. Moreover, administrators can use network performance testing tools like "iperf" to measure network bandwidth and latency between network endpoints. By running "iperf" server and client instances with appropriate options, administrators can conduct network performance tests and analyze the results to identify network congestion points and optimize network configuration for better performance. Additionally, administrators can use tracing and profiling tools like "strace" or "perf" to analyze the behavior and performance of individual processes or applications. For example, administrators can use "strace" to trace system calls and signals generated by a specific process and identify performance bottlenecks or inefficiencies in its execution. They can run "strace" commands with the "-p" option followed by the process ID to attach to a running process and trace its system calls in real-time. Similarly, administrators can use "perf" to profile CPU and memory usage of a process and identify hotspots or areas for optimization. They can run "perf" commands with appropriate options to collect performance data and generate reports for analysis. In summary, performance monitoring tools and techniques are essential for maintaining optimal system performance and user experience in IT environments. By leveraging tools like "top", "vmstat", "sysbench", "iperf", Nagios, Zabbix, "strace", and "perf", administrators can monitor system resources, identify performance bottlenecks, and optimize system configuration to deliver reliable and efficient IT services. System resource optimization strategies are crucial for maximizing the efficiency and performance of IT systems while minimizing resource wastage and costs. These strategies encompass various techniques and best practices aimed at optimizing CPU, memory, disk, and network utilization to ensure optimal system performance and responsiveness. One fundamental aspect of resource optimization is CPU utilization management, as high CPU usage can lead to performance degradation and system unresponsiveness. Administrators can monitor

CPU usage using commands like "top" or "ps" to identify processes consuming excessive CPU resources. By analyzing the output of these commands, administrators can pinpoint CPU-intensive processes and take appropriate actions to optimize their resource usage. For example, they can prioritize CPU-bound processes, adjust process scheduling priorities using the "nice" or "renice" commands, or optimize inefficient code to reduce CPU overhead. Additionally, administrators can leverage CPU affinity settings to assign specific CPU cores to critical processes, ensuring optimal CPU utilization and minimizing contention. Using tools like "taskset" in Linux, administrators can set CPU affinity for processes by specifying the CPU core or cores on which they should run. This helps distribute CPU load evenly across cores and prevents performance bottlenecks caused by core saturation. Furthermore, memory optimization is essential for maximizing system performance and responsiveness, especially in environments with limited memory resources. Administrators can monitor memory usage using commands like "free" or "vmstat" to assess available memory, used memory, and swap space utilization. By analyzing memory usage patterns, administrators can identify memory-hungry processes and optimize memory allocation to improve system performance. Techniques such as memory deduplication, compression, and caching can help reduce memory footprint and improve memory utilization efficiency. For example, administrators can enable memory deduplication features in virtualized environments to identify and eliminate duplicate memory pages, reducing memory overhead and improving virtual machine density. They can also configure memory compression mechanisms like zswap or zram to compress memory pages in RAM, reducing memory usage and swapping overhead. Additionally, administrators can optimize disk and storage resources to ensure efficient data access and minimize latency. Disk optimization techniques include disk partitioning, filesystem tuning, and storage tiering to improve disk performance and reliability. For example, administrators can use the "fdisk" or "parted" commands to create disk partitions aligned to the underlying storage device's physical block size, optimizing disk I/O performance. They can also tune filesystem parameters using utilities like "tune2fs" or "xfs_admin" to optimize filesystem performance and reduce fragmentation. Furthermore, administrators can implement storage tiering solutions to optimize data placement across different storage tiers based on access patterns and data importance. By using tools like "mdadm" or "lvm", administrators can create software RAID arrays or logical volumes spanning multiple storage devices with different performance characteristics, such as SSDs and HDDs, to improve overall storage performance and efficiency. Additionally, administrators can optimize network resources to ensure optimal network performance and bandwidth utilization. Network optimization techniques include bandwidth management, traffic shaping, and Quality of Service (QoS) configuration to prioritize network traffic and ensure critical applications receive adequate bandwidth and latency guarantees. Using tools like "tc" (Traffic Control) in Linux, administrators can implement traffic shaping policies to control bandwidth usage and prioritize traffic based on criteria such as source/destination IP address, port number, or packet size. They can configure QoS policies in network devices like routers and switches to prioritize traffic for real-time applications like VoIP or video conferencing over non-critical traffic like file downloads or web browsing. Moreover, administrators can optimize network protocols and settings to improve network performance and reduce latency. For example, they can enable features like TCP window scaling and selective acknowledgment (SACK) to improve TCP throughput and reliability in high-latency or high-bandwidth networks. Additionally, they can optimize network interface settings like MTU (Maximum Transmission Unit) and TCP buffer sizes to match the network characteristics and improve data transfer efficiency. In summary, system resource optimization strategies are essential for maximizing system performance and efficiency while minimizing resource wastage and costs. By implementing CPU utilization management, memory optimization, disk and storage optimization, and network optimization techniques, administrators can ensure optimal utilization of CPU, memory, disk, and network resources, resulting in improved system responsiveness, reliability, and user satisfaction.

Chapter 7: Advanced User and Group Management

User and group management commands and utilities are essential tools for system administrators to manage user accounts, groups, and permissions in Unix-based operating systems. These commands and utilities provide administrators with the ability to create, modify, and delete user accounts and groups, assign permissions, and manage user access to system resources. One fundamental command in user management is "useradd", which is used to create new user accounts on the system. Administrators can specify various options with the "useradd" command, such as the username, home directory, default shell, and user ID (UID). For example, to create a new user named "john" with the default options, administrators can simply run the command "useradd john". Additionally, administrators can use options like "-m" to create a home directory for the user, "-s" to specify the default shell, and "-u" to set a custom UID for the user. Once a user account is created, administrators can use the "passwd" command to set or change the password for the user. By running the command "passwd username", administrators can prompt the user to enter a new password and confirm it. The "passwd" command encrypts and stores the password securely in the system's password database, ensuring user account security. Moreover, administrators can use the "usermod" command to modify existing user accounts and change various attributes, such as the username, home directory, default shell, and group membership. For example, to change the default shell for a user named "mary" to "/bin/bash", administrators can run the command "usermod -s /bin/bash mary". Similarly, administrators can use the "userdel" command to delete user accounts from the system. When running the "userdel" command, administrators can specify options like "-r" to remove the user's home directory and mail spool, ensuring that all associated data is deleted along with the user account. In addition to managing user accounts, administrators often need to manage user groups to organize users and assign permissions efficiently. The "groupadd" command is used to create new groups on the system. Administrators can specify options like "-g" to set a custom GID (Group ID) for the group and "-r" to create a system group with a GID less than 1000. For example, to create a new group named "developers", administrators can run the command "groupadd developers". Once a group is created, administrators can use the "gpasswd" command to manage group membership and set group passwords. By running the command "gpasswd -a username groupname", administrators can add a user to a group, allowing the user to access resources and files associated with the group. Conversely, administrators can use the "gpasswd -d username groupname" command to remove a user from a group. Furthermore, administrators can use the "groupmod" command to modify existing groups and change attributes like the group name or GID. For example, to change the name of a group from "developers" to "engineers", administrators can run the command "groupmod -n engineers developers". Additionally, administrators can use the "groupdel" command to delete groups from the system. When running the "groupdel" command, administrators can specify options like "-r" to remove the group's associated files and directories. Alongside these basic commands, Unix-based operating systems offer graphical user interface (GUI) utilities for user and group management, such as "user-manager" and "gnome-system-tools" on Linux-based systems. These GUI utilities provide administrators with a user-friendly interface for managing user accounts, groups, and permissions, making it easier to perform common administrative tasks. However, many administrators prefer using CLI commands for user and group management due to their flexibility and scriptability, allowing for automation of repetitive tasks and bulk operations. In summary, user and group management commands and utilities are essential tools for system administrators to manage user accounts, groups, and permissions in Unix-based operating systems. By using commands like "useradd", "passwd", "usermod", "userdel", "groupadd", "gpasswd", "groupmod", and "groupdel", administrators can efficiently create, modify, and delete user accounts and groups, assign permissions, and manage user access to system resources, ensuring effective system administration and security.

Implementing Access Control Lists (ACLs) is a crucial aspect of managing file and directory permissions in Unix-based operating systems, providing administrators with fine-grained control over access to system resources. ACLs extend the traditional Unix permissions model by allowing administrators to define access permissions for specific users and groups beyond the basic read, write, and execute permissions. One of the primary commands used for ACL management is "getfacl", which displays the ACL entries for a file or directory. By running the command "getfacl filename", administrators can view the ACL entries associated with the specified file or directory, including the permissions assigned to users and groups. The output of the "getfacl" command typically includes entries for the owner, group owner, and additional user and group entries with their corresponding permissions. Additionally, administrators can use the "setfacl" command to modify or set ACL entries for files and directories. The "setfacl" command allows administrators to specify permissions for specific users and groups, granting or revoking read, write, and execute permissions as needed. For example, to grant read and write permissions to a user named "alice" on a file named "document.txt", administrators can run the command "setfacl -m u:alice:rw document.txt". Similarly, administrators can use the "setfacl" command to grant permissions to groups by specifying the group identifier (GID) preceded by "g:". For instance, to grant read and execute permissions to a group named "developers" on a directory named "projects", administrators can run the command "setfacl -m g:developers:rx projects". Moreover, administrators can use the "setfacl" command to set default ACL entries for newly created files and directories within a specific directory. By adding the "-d" option to the "setfacl" command, administrators can set default ACL entries that will be inherited by all files and directories created within the specified directory. For example, to set default ACL entries for a directory named "shared" to grant read and write permissions to a group named "users", administrators can run the command "setfacl -m d:g:users:rw shared". This ensures that all files and directories created within the "shared" directory inherit the specified default ACL entries. Additionally, administrators can use the "chmod" command in conjunction with ACLs to manage traditional Unix permissions alongside ACL entries. The "chmod" command allows administrators to modify the traditional Unix permissions for files and directories, while ACL entries provide additional granularity for access control. For example, administrators can use the "chmod" command to set the traditional Unix permissions to restrict access to a file or directory, and then use the "setfacl" command to grant specific users or groups additional access permissions beyond the traditional permissions. Furthermore, administrators can leverage ACLs to implement more complex access control policies, such as role-based access control (RBAC) or attribute-based access control (ABAC). With ACLs, administrators can define access permissions based on user attributes, such as user roles, department memberships, or project affiliations, allowing for more dynamic and flexible access control policies. This enables administrators to tailor access permissions to specific user roles or contexts, ensuring that users have the appropriate level of access to system resources based on their roles and responsibilities. In summary, implementing Access Control Lists (ACLs) is a powerful technique for managing file and directory permissions in Unix-based operating systems, providing administrators with fine-grained control over access to system resources. By using commands like "getfacl" and "setfacl", administrators can view and modify ACL entries to grant or revoke access permissions for specific users and groups, extending the traditional Unix permissions model to support more complex access control requirements. Additionally, ACLs enable administrators to implement advanced access control policies, such as role-based access control (RBAC) or attribute-based access control (ABAC), allowing for more dynamic and flexible access control configurations tailored to the organization's needs.

Chapter 8: High Availability and Fault Tolerance Techniques

Implementing redundancy and failover is essential in ensuring high availability and reliability of systems and services, particularly in critical environments where downtime can result in significant financial losses or operational disruptions. Redundancy involves duplicating critical components or resources to provide backup in case of failure, while failover mechanisms automatically switch to redundant components or systems when primary ones fail. One common approach to implementing redundancy is through the use of redundant hardware components, such as redundant power supplies, network interfaces, and storage arrays. For example, servers in a data center can be equipped with dual power supplies, each connected to a separate power source, to ensure uninterrupted power delivery in case one power supply fails. Similarly, network switches can be configured with redundant uplink connections to multiple routers or switches, allowing traffic to be rerouted automatically in case of link failure. Additionally, storage systems can be configured with redundant disk arrays, such as RAID (Redundant Array of Independent Disks), to protect against data loss in the event of disk failures. RAID configurations, such as RAID 1 (mirroring) or RAID 5 (striping with parity), provide redundancy by storing data across multiple disks, allowing data to be reconstructed even if one or more disks fail. In addition to hardware redundancy, software-based redundancy mechanisms can also be implemented to ensure high availability of applications and services. One common approach is the use of load balancers, which distribute incoming traffic across multiple servers or instances to ensure optimal performance and reliability. Load balancers monitor the health and availability of backend servers and automatically reroute traffic away from failed or overloaded servers to healthy ones. For example, popular load balancing solutions like Nginx or HAProxy can be deployed in front of web servers to distribute incoming HTTP requests across multiple backend servers, ensuring that the application remains accessible even if individual servers fail. Furthermore, clustering technologies can be used to implement failover for critical services by grouping multiple servers or nodes into a cluster and synchronizing data and state information across the cluster. In the event of a failure, services can automatically failover to standby nodes within the cluster, ensuring uninterrupted service availability. For example, database clustering solutions like MySQL Cluster or PostgreSQL Replication can be deployed to replicate data across multiple database nodes and automatically failover to standby nodes in case of database server failures. Similarly, application clustering solutions like Microsoft Failover Cluster or Pacemaker on Linux can be used to create high availability clusters for applications and services, ensuring continuous operation in the event of server or application failures. Moreover, cloud computing platforms offer built-in redundancy and failover capabilities to ensure high availability of applications and services deployed in the cloud. Cloud providers like Amazon Web Services (AWS), Microsoft Azure, and Google Cloud Platform (GCP) offer services such as Auto Scaling, Elastic Load Balancing, and managed database services with built-in replication and failover capabilities. By leveraging these cloud services, organizations can ensure that their applications and services remain available and resilient to failures without the need for complex infrastructure management. In summary, implementing redundancy and failover mechanisms is crucial for ensuring high availability and reliability of systems and services in today's digital landscape. By deploying redundant hardware components, such as power supplies, network interfaces, and storage arrays, organizations can minimize the risk of hardware failures and ensure uninterrupted operation of critical infrastructure. Additionally, software-based redundancy mechanisms, such as load balancers, clustering, and cloud-based services, provide automated failover and high availability for applications and services, further enhancing resilience and minimizing downtime. Load balancing and clustering technologies play a pivotal role in ensuring the scalability, availability, and reliability of modern IT infrastructures. Load balancing involves distributing incoming network traffic across multiple servers or resources to optimize resource utilization and prevent overload on any single server. One of the most commonly used load balancing techniques is Round Robin DNS, which distributes incoming requests across a pool of servers by rotating the IP addresses returned in DNS responses. This approach is simple to implement but lacks intelligence and does not consider server health or capacity. Alternatively, organizations often deploy dedicated load balancers, such as HAProxy or Nginx, which offer more sophisticated algorithms for distributing traffic based on factors like server health, response times, and server capacity. These load balancers continuously monitor the health and performance of backend servers and route traffic accordingly, ensuring optimal performance and availability. For example, administrators can configure HAProxy to use the Least Connections algorithm, which directs traffic to the server with the fewest active connections, or the Weighted

Round Robin algorithm, which assigns weights to servers based on their capacity or performance. Moreover, clustering technologies enable the grouping of multiple servers or nodes into a single logical entity to provide high availability, fault tolerance, and scalability for applications and services. A popular clustering solution for databases is MySQL Cluster, which enables synchronous replication of data across multiple nodes to ensure data consistency and availability. Administrators can deploy MySQL Cluster to create a distributed database cluster that spans multiple geographic regions, providing high availability and disaster recovery capabilities. Similarly, in the realm of web servers and applications, administrators can deploy clustering solutions like Microsoft Windows Server Failover Clustering or Pacemaker on Linux to create high availability clusters that automatically failover to standby nodes in case of server failures. These clustering solutions enable organizations to ensure continuous operation of critical applications and services, even in the face of hardware failures or network outages. Additionally, cloud providers offer managed load balancing and clustering services that simplify the deployment and management of scalable and highly available applications in the cloud. For example, Amazon Web Services (AWS) offers Elastic Load Balancing (ELB), which automatically distributes incoming traffic across multiple EC2 instances or containers, ensuring high availability and fault tolerance. Similarly, Azure Load Balancer and Google Cloud Load Balancing provide similar functionality for distributing traffic across virtual machines or Kubernetes clusters in the respective cloud platforms. Furthermore, container orchestration platforms like Kubernetes enable organizations to deploy and manage containerized applications at scale, leveraging built-in load balancing and clustering capabilities. Kubernetes automatically distributes incoming traffic across pods (groups of containers) using a built-in load balancer called kube-proxy, ensuring optimal performance and high availability of containerized applications. Additionally, Kubernetes supports features like horizontal pod autoscaling, which automatically adjusts the number of pod replicas based on resource utilization, enabling organizations to scale applications dynamically in response to changing workloads. In summary, load balancing and clustering technologies are indispensable tools for ensuring the scalability, availability, and reliability of modern IT infrastructures. By deploying load balancers and clustering solutions, organizations can distribute traffic intelligently, optimize resource utilization, and ensure continuous operation of critical applications and services, whether deployed on-premises or in the cloud.

BOOK 4

IOS DEMYSTIFIED

EXPERT INSIGHTS INTO APPLE'S OPERATING SYSTEM

ROB BOTWRIGHT

Chapter 1: Introduction to iOS: Evolution and Core Principles

The history of iOS traces back to the inception of the iPhone, Apple's iconic smartphone that revolutionized the mobile industry upon its release in 2007. Developed by Apple Inc., iOS, initially known as iPhone OS, was designed to power the iPhone and provide users with a seamless and intuitive mobile experience. The first version of iPhone OS, iOS 1.0, introduced several groundbreaking features, including the revolutionary multi-touch interface, Safari web browser, and integration with iTunes for music and media playback. Over the years, iOS has undergone significant evolution and refinement, with each new version introducing innovative features and enhancements to improve performance, security, and user experience. iOS 2.0, released in 2008, marked a significant milestone with the introduction of the App Store, allowing users to download and install third-party applications directly onto their devices. This opened up a new era of mobile computing, unleashing a wave of creativity and innovation among developers who created a vast ecosystem of apps spanning various categories, from games and entertainment to productivity and utility. With iOS 3.0, released in 2009, Apple introduced several key features, including copy and paste, MMS support, and Spotlight search, further enhancing the functionality and versatility of the platform. iOS 4.0, launched in 2010, brought multitasking capabilities to the iPhone, enabling users to switch between apps and perform background tasks more efficiently. This release also introduced FaceTime, Apple's video calling feature, and iBooks, Apple's digital bookstore, expanding the iPhone's capabilities beyond communication and entertainment to include education and productivity. Subsequent iterations of iOS continued to build upon this foundation, introducing new features and improvements to keep pace with the evolving needs and expectations of users. iOS 5.0, released in 2011, introduced iCloud, Apple's cloud storage and synchronization service, enabling seamless integration and synchronization of content across multiple devices. This release also introduced Notification Center, iMessage, and Siri, Apple's voice-activated virtual assistant, further enhancing the iPhone's capabilities and usability. iOS 6.0, launched in 2012, brought several enhancements to key features, including Maps,

Siri, and Safari, as well as the introduction of Passbook, Apple's digital wallet for storing tickets, boarding passes, and loyalty cards. However, it also faced criticism for its Apple Maps application, which was plagued by inaccuracies and usability issues. With iOS 7.0, released in 2013, Apple introduced a radical redesign of the iOS user interface, featuring a flatter and more colorful design language, as well as a host of new features and enhancements, including Control Center, AirDrop, and iTunes Radio. This release marked a significant departure from previous versions of iOS and signaled Apple's commitment to innovation and evolution. Subsequent releases of iOS continued to refine the user experience and introduce new features and capabilities, including enhancements to security and privacy, improvements to performance and battery life, and support for emerging technologies such as augmented reality and machine learning. Today, iOS stands as one of the most advanced and feature-rich mobile operating systems in the world, powering millions of devices and empowering users to do more than ever before. With its intuitive interface, robust security features, and seamless integration with other Apple products and services, iOS continues to set the standard for mobile computing and shape the future of technology. The core principles of iOS development are rooted in Apple's Human Interface Guidelines (HIG), a comprehensive set of design principles and best practices that govern the creation of apps for the iOS platform. These guidelines, meticulously crafted by Apple, serve as a blueprint for developers to create apps that deliver a consistent and intuitive user experience across all iOS devices, including iPhone, iPad, and iPod touch. Adhering to these principles is essential for creating apps that not only look great but also feel natural and intuitive to use, enhancing user satisfaction and engagement. The HIG covers various aspects of app design, including layout, navigation, typography, color, and interaction, providing developers with guidance on how to create apps that are both visually appealing and easy to navigate. One of the key principles outlined in the HIG is clarity, which emphasizes the importance of presenting information and functionality in a clear and easily understandable manner. This includes using concise and descriptive language, avoiding jargon or technical terms, and providing clear visual cues to guide users through the app. For example, developers can use descriptive labels and icons to convey the purpose and function of on-screen controls, ensuring that users can quickly understand how to interact with the app. Another fundamental principle of iOS development is simplicity, which advocates for streamlining the user interface and minimizing complexity to enhance usability. This involves focusing on essential features and functionality, avoiding clutter and unnecessary visual elements, and designing for ease of use and efficiency. Developers can achieve simplicity by prioritizing content and functionality based on user needs, removing extraneous elements that detract from the user experience, and adopting a minimalist design aesthetic. For instance, developers can use whitespace to create visual breathing room and improve readability, prioritize primary actions and content over secondary or tertiary elements, and use consistent and predictable navigation patterns to guide users through the app. Consistency is another core principle of iOS development, emphasizing the importance of maintaining a unified and cohesive user experience across all aspects of the app. This includes using standard iOS controls, behaviors, and interactions, adhering to platform conventions and guidelines, and ensuring that the app's design is consistent with the overall look and feel of iOS. By leveraging familiar design patterns and interactions, developers can create apps that feel instantly familiar to users, reducing the learning curve and increasing usability. For example, developers can use standard iOS navigation patterns such as tab bars, navigation bars, and modal presentations to provide users with a consistent and predictable way to navigate through the app. Accessibility is also a fundamental principle of iOS development, emphasizing the importance of designing apps that are inclusive and accessible to users of all abilities. This involves designing apps with accessibility features in mind, such as support for VoiceOver, Dynamic Type, and Switch Control, ensuring that users with disabilities can access and interact with the app effectively. Developers can enhance accessibility by using semantic markup, providing alternative text for images and other non-text elements, and testing their apps with assistive technologies to identify and address accessibility issues. In summary, the core principles of iOS development outlined in Apple's Human Interface Guidelines are essential for creating apps that deliver a seamless and intuitive user experience. By prioritizing clarity, simplicity, consistency, and accessibility, developers can create apps that not only look great but also feel natural and intuitive to use, enhancing user satisfaction and engagement.

Chapter 2: Navigating the iOS Interface: From Home Screen to Settings

The Home Screen is the central hub of interaction on iOS devices, serving as the launching pad for accessing apps, widgets, and other essential features. Understanding the layout and navigation of the Home Screen is fundamental to navigating iOS devices efficiently and maximizing productivity. At the core of the Home Screen is the grid of app icons, arranged in rows and columns, representing installed apps and providing quick access to their functionality. Users can customize the layout of their Home Screen by rearranging app icons, creating folders to organize apps into categories, and adding widgets for at-a-glance information and quick access to key features. To rearrange app icons on the Home Screen, users can tap and hold an app icon until it enters editing mode, then drag it to a new location or drop it onto another app icon to create a folder. Users can also tap and hold an app icon to access additional options, such as deleting the app, moving it to a different screen or folder, or accessing app-specific shortcuts and widgets. Additionally, users can use the App Library, a feature introduced in iOS 14, to automatically organize apps into categories and access them via a searchable interface. The Home Screen also includes a dock at the bottom of the screen, which provides quick access to frequently used apps and can be customized to include up to six app icons. Users can customize the dock by dragging app icons onto or off of the dock, rearranging them as desired. The dock also includes a persistent area for recently used apps, making it easy to switch between apps without navigating back to the Home Screen. Beyond app icons, the Home Screen can also display widgets, which provide at-a-glance information and quick access to key features from supported apps. Widgets come in various sizes and can be placed anywhere on the Home Screen or in the Today View, a dedicated space accessible by swiping right from the left edge of the Home Screen. Users can customize widgets by tapping and holding an empty area of the Home Screen to enter jiggle mode, then tapping the "+" button in the top-left corner to access the widget gallery. From there, users can select a widget, choose its size, and add it to the Home Screen or Today View. Widgets can display a wide range of information, including weather forecasts, calendar events, reminders, news headlines, and more, providing users with valuable insights and quick access to key app features. In addition to app icons and widgets, the Home Screen also includes a search bar at the top, allowing users to quickly search for apps, contacts, documents, and other content on their device. Users can access the search bar by swiping down from the middle of the Home Screen or by swiping right from the left edge of the Home Screen to access the Today View and then swiping down. From there, users can type their query using the on-screen keyboard or use dictation to perform a voice search. The search bar also provides suggestions as users type, helping them quickly find what they're looking for. In summary, exploring the Home Screen layout and navigation is essential for mastering iOS devices and maximizing productivity. By understanding how to customize app icons, rearrange the dock, add widgets, and use the search bar effectively, users can tailor their Home Screen to suit their needs and access apps and features quickly and efficiently.

Customizing iOS settings is essential for tailoring the user experience to personal preferences and optimizing device efficiency. iOS offers a wide range of settings that allow users to customize various aspects of their device, from appearance and accessibility to privacy and security. By exploring and adjusting these settings, users can create a personalized iOS experience that suits their needs and enhances their productivity. One of the most basic and essential settings to customize is the wallpaper, which allows users to change the background image of their device's Home Screen and Lock Screen. To change the wallpaper on an iOS device, users can navigate to "Settings" > "Wallpaper," then choose a new wallpaper from the available options or select an image from their photo library. Users can also adjust the appearance of their device by enabling or disabling features such as Dark Mode, which changes the color scheme of the interface to a darker palette for improved readability in low-light conditions. To enable Dark Mode, users can navigate to "Settings" > "Display & Brightness" and toggle the "Dark" option. Additionally, users can customize the appearance of text and buttons by adjusting the text size, bold text, and button shapes in the "Display & Brightness" settings. Another important aspect of customizing iOS settings is optimizing device performance and battery life. iOS provides several settings that allow users to manage background app refresh, location services, and notifications to conserve battery life and improve performance. For example, users can disable background app refresh for specific apps or enable Low Power Mode to reduce power consumption when the battery is low. To manage background app refresh settings, users can navigate to "Settings" > "General" > "Background App Refresh," then choose whether to enable or disable background app refresh for each app individually or disable it entirely. Users can also manage location services settings to control which apps have access to their device's location data and when it is accessed. To manage location services settings, users can navigate to "Settings" > "Privacy" > "Location Services," then choose whether to enable or disable location services for each app individually or disable it entirely. Additionally, users can customize notifications settings to control which apps can send notifications and how they are displayed. To manage notifications settings, users can navigate to "Settings" > "Notifications," then choose the desired app from the list and adjust the notification settings as desired, including enabling or disabling notifications, choosing notification styles, and setting notification preferences. In addition to appearance and performance settings, iOS also offers a range of accessibility settings that allow users to customize their device to meet their individual needs. These settings include options for adjusting text size, enhancing contrast, enabling spoken content, and configuring assistive touch gestures. To access accessibility settings, users can navigate to "Settings" > "Accessibility," then explore the various options available to customize their device's accessibility features. Furthermore, iOS provides robust privacy and security settings that allow users to control their device's privacy and security settings. These settings include options for managing app permissions, restricting access to sensitive data, and enabling features such as Face ID or Touch ID for device authentication. To access privacy and security settings, users can navigate to "Settings" > "Privacy" or "Settings" > "Face ID & Passcode" or "Touch ID & Passcode," then configure the desired settings as needed. In summary, customizing iOS settings is essential for personalizing the user experience, optimizing device performance and battery life, enhancing accessibility, and ensuring privacy and security. By exploring and adjusting the wide range of settings available on iOS devices, users can create a customized iOS experience that meets their individual needs and preferences. Exploring essential iOS features such as Siri, Control Center, Notifications, and more provides users with a comprehensive understanding of the capabilities and functionalities available on their iOS devices.

These features are integral to the iOS experience, offering convenience, efficiency, and customization options to enhance productivity and streamline daily tasks. Among the most prominent features is Siri, Apple's intelligent virtual assistant, which allows users to perform various tasks using voice commands. With Siri, users can send messages, set reminders, make phone calls, search the web, and control smart home devices, among other functions. To activate Siri, users can either say "Hey Siri" followed by their command or press and hold the Home button (or the side button on devices without a Home button) until Siri appears. Once activated, users can speak their command or question, and Siri will respond accordingly. Siri can also be customized by navigating to "Settings" > "Siri & Search," where users can enable or disable Siri, configure language and voice settings, and manage Siri suggestions and shortcuts. Control Center is another essential iOS feature that provides quick access to commonly used settings and controls. It allows users to adjust settings such as Wi-Fi, Bluetooth, brightness, and volume, as well as access shortcuts for functions like flashlight, camera, and screen mirroring. To access Control Center, users can swipe down from the top-right corner of the screen (or swipe up from the bottom edge on older iPhone models). They can then tap on the desired control to toggle it on or off or perform a quick action. Control Center can be customized by navigating to "Settings" > "Control Center," where users can add or remove controls and rearrange their order. Notifications play a crucial role in keeping users informed and up-to-date with important information and updates. iOS provides a unified notification system that delivers notifications from apps, messages, emails, and more in a centralized location. Users can view and manage notifications by swiping down from the top of the screen to access the Notification Center. From there, they can review notifications, clear them individually or in groups, and customize notification settings for each app. To customize notification settings, users can navigate to "Settings" > "Notifications," where they can enable or disable notifications for each app, choose notification styles, and configure additional options such as notification grouping and notification previews. Another essential iOS feature is the App Store, which serves as the primary source for downloading and installing apps on iOS devices. With the App Store, users can discover and download millions of apps across various categories, including games, productivity tools, social networking apps, and more. To access the App Store, users can tap on the App Store icon on their device's Home Screen. They can then browse featured apps, search for specific apps using the search bar, and explore curated lists and collections. Additionally, users can manage their app downloads and updates by navigating to the "Updates" tab in the App Store, where they can view available updates and install them individually or all at once. In addition to these features, iOS offers a wide range of other essential functionalities, such as iCloud, which provides cloud storage and synchronization services for photos, videos, documents, and more; FaceTime, which allows users to make video and audio calls to other iOS and macOS devices; and Apple Pay, which enables secure and convenient payments using supported devices. By familiarizing themselves with these essential iOS features, users can make the most of their iOS devices and optimize their user experience for greater efficiency, productivity, and enjoyment.

Chapter 3: Exploring Essential iOS Apps and Features

An in-depth exploration of the built-in iOS apps is crucial for mastering the functionality and versatility of iOS devices. These native applications offer a wide range of features and capabilities designed to enhance communication, productivity, and entertainment. Among the most prominent built-in iOS apps are Messages, Mail, Safari, and more, each offering unique functionality tailored to meet various user needs. Messages serves as the primary messaging app on iOS devices, allowing users to send text messages, photos, videos, and audio messages to contacts via SMS, iMessage, or third-party messaging services. Users can also engage in group chats, share their location, and use various interactive features such as Animoji and Memoji. To compose a message in Messages, users can open the app, tap the new message icon, then select a contact or enter a phone number or email address. They can then type their message using the on-screen keyboard or use dictation to input text. Additionally, users can access various message settings by navigating to "Settings" > "Messages," where they can configure options such as iMessage, message forwarding, and message filtering. Mail is another essential built-in iOS app that provides users with a powerful email client for managing their email accounts. With Mail, users can send, receive, and organize emails from multiple accounts, including iCloud, Gmail, Yahoo, and more. The app offers features such as threaded conversations, VIP contacts, and customizable mailboxes, allowing users to stay organized and efficient with their email communication. To set up an email account in Mail, users can navigate to "Settings" > "Mail" > "Accounts," then select "Add Account" and follow the prompts to enter their email address and password. Safari is the default web browser on iOS devices, offering a fast, secure, and user-friendly browsing experience. With Safari, users can browse the web, bookmark favorite sites, open multiple tabs, and access advanced features such as Reader View, which provides a distraction-free reading experience, and Private Browsing mode, which prevents browsing history and data from being stored. To open a new tab in Safari, users can tap the tab icon in the bottom-right corner of the screen, then tap the "+" button to open a new tab. They can then enter a URL or search term in the address bar to navigate to a website. Additionally, users can customize Safari settings by navigating to "Settings" > "Safari," where they can configure options such as search engine preferences, content blockers, and autofill settings. Other notable built-in iOS apps include Photos, which allows users to capture, organize, and edit photos and videos; Calendar, which provides a comprehensive scheduling and time management tool; and Maps, which offers detailed maps, directions, and location-based services. Each of these apps plays a vital role in the iOS ecosystem, contributing to a seamless and integrated user experience. By familiarizing themselves with the features and capabilities of these built-in apps, users can unlock the full potential of their iOS devices and streamline their daily tasks and activities.

Chapter 4: Understanding iOS Security and Privacy Measures

Understanding the iOS security architecture is crucial for ensuring the protection of user data and the integrity of the operating system. At the core of iOS security is its sandboxing mechanism, which restricts the access that apps have to system resources and user data. The sandbox isolates each app within its own container, preventing it from accessing files and resources belonging to other apps or the system. This isolation ensures that even if one app is compromised, it cannot access sensitive information from other apps or the system. To enforce sandboxing, iOS assigns a unique identifier, known as the sandbox directory, to each app. This directory serves as the app's private storage space, where it can store its files and data without interference from other apps. Additionally, iOS implements strong encryption measures to protect user data both at rest and in transit. File-Level Encryption ensures that all user data stored on the device is encrypted using AES-256 encryption, with keys derived from the user's passcode. This encryption extends to all files and data stored in the device's file system, including photos, videos, documents, and app data. Furthermore, iOS utilizes Secure Enclave, a dedicated coprocessor within the device's processor, to manage encryption keys and perform cryptographic operations securely. The Secure Enclave stores encryption keys in a tamper-resistant manner, ensuring that they cannot be accessed or compromised by malicious software or hardware. To ensure the integrity of app data, iOS requires all apps to be digitally signed with a unique certificate issued by Apple. This code signing process verifies the authenticity and integrity of the app, ensuring that it has not been tampered with or modified since its release. Additionally, iOS employs runtime protections, such as Address Space Layout Randomization (ASLR) and Data Execution Prevention (DEP), to prevent buffer overflow attacks and other memory-related vulnerabilities. ASLR randomizes the memory address space used by apps, making it difficult for attackers to predict the location of sensitive data or code. DEP prevents apps from executing code stored in non-executable memory regions, reducing the risk of code injection attacks. Another critical component of iOS security is the Keychain, a secure storage mechanism for sensitive information such as passwords, cryptographic keys, and certificates. The Keychain encrypts this information using a combination of the device's unique identifier and the user's passcode, ensuring that it remains protected even if the device is compromised. Apps can securely access and store sensitive data in the Keychain using the Keychain Services API, which provides a set of functions for managing Keychain items. This API allows apps to create, read, update, and delete Keychain items, as well as perform cryptographic operations such as encryption, decryption, and digital signatures. Additionally, iOS provides comprehensive security features for network communications, including support for secure protocols such as TLS/SSL and VPN. Apps can use these protocols to encrypt network traffic and establish secure connections with servers, protecting sensitive data from eavesdropping and tampering. Furthermore, iOS includes built-in security controls such as App Transport Security (ATS), which enforces best practices for secure network communication, and Network Extension Framework, which allows apps to extend the functionality of the built-in VPN and firewall features. Overall, the iOS security architecture is designed to provide multiple layers of protection against a wide range of threats, including malware, data breaches, and unauthorized access. By leveraging sandboxing, encryption, code signing, runtime protections, and secure storage mechanisms such as the Keychain, iOS ensures the confidentiality, integrity, and availability of user data and the operating system.

Privacy settings and permissions management play a critical role in safeguarding user data and maintaining user trust within the iOS ecosystem. iOS offers granular control over privacy settings, empowering users to determine which apps have access to their personal information and device features. One fundamental aspect of privacy management in iOS is the control over app permissions, which regulate an app's access to sensitive data and functionalities. Users can manage app permissions directly through the Settings app or during the initial setup of an app. By navigating to Settings > Privacy, users can review and modify permissions related to location services, camera, microphone, contacts, photos, and more. For instance, to grant or revoke location access for specific apps, users can go to Settings > Privacy > Location Services and toggle the switch next to each app's name. Similarly, users can manage permissions for accessing photos, contacts, camera, and other resources under the corresponding Privacy settings.

Additionally, iOS employs prompts to request user consent before granting apps access to sensitive data or features. When an app attempts to access protected resources for the first time, such as the camera, microphone, or location services, iOS displays a permission prompt, requesting the user's authorization. The user can choose to grant or deny access, and their decision is recorded in the app's permissions settings. iOS also offers additional privacy features such as App Tracking Transparency (ATT), which gives users more control over app tracking and data collection for personalized advertising. With ATT, apps are required to obtain explicit user consent before tracking their activity across other apps and websites for targeted advertising purposes. Users can manage app tracking preferences by going to Settings > Privacy > Tracking and toggling the "Allow Apps to Request to Track" switch. Furthermore, iOS provides enhanced privacy protections through features like Private Relay and Hide My Email. Private Relay is a feature of iCloud+ that encrypts and anonymizes internet traffic, preventing network providers and websites from tracking users' browsing activity. Hide My Email allows users to create unique, randomly generated email addresses that forward messages to their primary inbox, protecting their personal email address from being shared with third parties. These privacy-enhancing features demonstrate Apple's commitment to prioritizing user privacy and security. In addition to managing app permissions and privacy settings, iOS includes robust security measures to protect user data from unauthorized access and breaches. iOS devices employ hardware-backed encryption to safeguard sensitive information stored on the device, such as passwords, payment data, and health records. This encryption ensures that even if an unauthorized individual gains physical access to the device, they cannot access or decrypt the data without the user's passcode or biometric authentication. iOS also implements strong authentication mechanisms, including Face ID and Touch ID, to prevent unauthorized access to the device and sensitive data. These biometric authentication methods provide a secure and convenient way for users to unlock their devices, authenticate app purchases, and authorize sensitive transactions. Additionally, iOS offers features like two-factor authentication (2FA) and account recovery to further secure user accounts and prevent unauthorized access to iCloud, App Store, and other Apple services. With 2FA enabled, users receive a verification code on a trusted device or phone number whenever they sign in to their Apple ID from a new device or browser. This additional layer of security helps prevent unauthorized access, even if an attacker obtains the user's password. Overall, privacy settings and permissions management are integral components of iOS's comprehensive approach to user privacy and security. By empowering users to control their data and manage app permissions, iOS fosters trust and confidence in the platform while ensuring that user privacy remains paramount.

Chapter 5: Mastering iCloud and Data Synchronization

iCloud is a comprehensive cloud storage and synchronization service provided by Apple, designed to seamlessly integrate with iOS, macOS, and other Apple devices. It offers users a convenient and secure way to store their data, back up their devices, and synchronize content across multiple devices. At its core, iCloud provides users with a centralized repository for storing various types of data, including photos, videos, documents, music, app data, and more. By leveraging iCloud, users can access their files and media from any supported device, regardless of their location. To begin using iCloud, users need to sign in with their Apple ID on their iOS device or Mac computer. Once signed in, they can enable iCloud features such as iCloud Drive, Photos, Contacts, Calendar, Notes, Reminders, and more. iCloud Drive serves as a central hub for storing and organizing files and folders in the cloud. Users can upload documents, presentations, spreadsheets, and other files to iCloud Drive directly from their device or computer. To access iCloud Drive on iOS, users can open the Files app, while on macOS, they can access it through Finder. Additionally, iCloud Drive seamlessly integrates with third-party apps, allowing users to save and access files across different applications. iCloud Photos provides users with a convenient way to store, organize, and access their photo and video libraries across all their devices. When enabled, iCloud Photos automatically uploads photos and videos from the user's device to their iCloud account, making them accessible from any other device signed in with the same Apple ID. Users can manage their photo library, create albums, and share photos with friends and family directly from the Photos app on iOS or macOS. Furthermore, iCloud Photos includes features like Shared Albums, which allow users to collaborate and share photos with others, and Memories, which automatically curates and presents users with personalized photo collections based on time, location, and people. iCloud Backup offers users a convenient and automatic way to back up their iOS and macOS devices to the cloud. When enabled, iCloud Backup automatically backs up the user's device data, including app data, settings, messages, photos, and more, to their iCloud account on a regular basis. This ensures that users have a secure and up-to-date backup of their device in case of loss, damage, or upgrade.

To enable iCloud Backup on iOS, users can go to Settings > [their name] > iCloud > iCloud Backup, and toggle the switch. On macOS, users can enable iCloud Backup through System Preferences > Apple ID > iCloud > iCloud Backup. Additionally, iCloud Backup allows users to restore their device from a backup quickly and easily during the setup process or after a device reset. iCloud also offers synchronization features for various types of data, including contacts, calendars, reminders, notes, and Safari bookmarks. By enabling iCloud sync for these items, users can ensure that their data stays consistent across all their devices. For example, when a user adds a new contact on their iPhone, it automatically syncs to their other devices, such as their iPad or Mac. Similarly, changes made to calendar events, reminders, notes, or Safari bookmarks are synchronized across all devices in real-time. This seamless synchronization ensures that users have access to their latest information wherever they go. In addition to storing and syncing user data, iCloud offers additional features such as Find My, which helps users locate lost or stolen devices, and iCloud Keychain, which securely stores and syncs passwords and payment information across devices. With its comprehensive set of features and seamless integration with Apple devices, iCloud provides users with a powerful and convenient solution for storing, backing up, and synchronizing their data across all their devices. Whether it's accessing files on the go, sharing photos with friends, or ensuring data security and peace of mind, iCloud plays a central role in the Apple ecosystem. Data synchronization across iOS devices is a crucial aspect of the user experience, allowing users to seamlessly access and update their information across all their Apple devices. One of the primary methods for implementing data synchronization on iOS devices is through iCloud, Apple's cloud storage and synchronization service. iCloud offers a range of features designed to facilitate data synchronization, including iCloud Drive, iCloud Photos, iCloud Backup, and iCloud Sync for various types of data such as contacts, calendars, reminders, notes, and more. To enable data synchronization across iOS devices using iCloud, users first need to ensure that iCloud is set up and configured on each of their devices. This involves signing in with the same Apple ID on all devices and enabling iCloud features such as iCloud Drive, iCloud Photos, and iCloud Backup. Once iCloud is set up, data synchronization occurs automatically in the background, ensuring that changes made on one device are reflected on all other devices associated with the same iCloud account. For example, when a user adds a new contact on their iPhone, it is automatically synchronized to their other iOS devices, such as their iPad or Mac. Similarly, changes made to calendar events, reminders, notes, or Safari bookmarks are synchronized across all devices in real-time. This seamless synchronization ensures that users have access to their latest information wherever they go. iCloud also offers synchronization for third-party apps through iCloud Sync, allowing developers to incorporate iCloud into their apps to sync data across multiple devices. Developers can leverage iCloud Sync to synchronize various types of app data, such as settings, preferences, documents, and user-generated content. To implement iCloud Sync in an iOS app, developers need to integrate the iCloud framework into their app and use iCloud APIs to manage the synchronization process. This involves configuring the app's iCloud capabilities in the app's Xcode project settings, handling conflicts and data consistency issues, and managing the synchronization of data between the app and iCloud. By leveraging iCloud Sync, developers can provide users with a seamless and consistent experience across all their devices, ensuring that their app's data is always up-to-date and accessible. In addition to iCloud, developers can also implement custom data synchronization solutions using other technologies such as iCloud Core Data or CloudKit. iCloud Core Data is a framework provided by Apple that allows developers to sync Core Data databases across multiple devices using iCloud. Developers can enable iCloud Core Data in their app's Xcode project settings and configure it to automatically sync changes to the Core Data database to iCloud. CloudKit is another option for implementing custom data synchronization in iOS apps. CloudKit provides a scalable and secure backend infrastructure for syncing app data across devices, handling user authentication, data storage, and data synchronization. Developers can use CloudKit APIs to store and sync app data in the cloud and manage data changes and conflicts. Overall, implementing data synchronization across iOS devices is essential for providing users with a seamless and consistent experience across all their Apple devices. Whether using iCloud or custom synchronization solutions, developers can ensure that users have access to their latest information wherever they go, enhancing the usability and functionality of their iOS apps.

Chapter 6: Developing iOS Apps: An Overview for Beginners

Introduction to iOS app development encompasses a wide array of tools and technologies, each playing a pivotal role in creating robust and user-friendly applications for Apple's mobile platform. At the forefront of iOS app development is Xcode, Apple's integrated development environment (IDE) designed specifically for building applications for iOS, macOS, watchOS, and tvOS. To begin developing iOS apps, developers typically start by downloading and installing Xcode from the Mac App Store. Once installed, developers can launch Xcode and start a new project by selecting the "Create a new Xcode project" option from the welcome window or the File menu. This opens a project template chooser where developers can select from various project templates, including Single View App, Master-Detail App, Tabbed App, and more. After choosing a template, developers need to specify the project's name, organization identifier, language (Swift or Objective-C), and other project settings before clicking the "Next" button to create the project. Xcode provides a comprehensive set of tools and features to streamline the iOS app development process, including code editing, debugging, interface design, asset management, and project management. One of the key components of Xcode is Interface Builder, a graphical user interface (GUI) design tool integrated into Xcode that allows developers to visually design app interfaces using drag-and-drop components. Interface Builder enables developers to create and customize user interfaces for their iOS apps by arranging UI elements such as buttons, labels, text fields, and images on a canvas and configuring their properties, constraints, and behavior. Developers can switch between the code editor and Interface Builder to seamlessly transition between writing code and designing interfaces, facilitating rapid prototyping and iteration. Alongside Xcode and Interface Builder, Swift serves as the primary programming language for iOS app development. Swift is a powerful and intuitive programming language developed by Apple that offers modern syntax, type safety, memory management, and performance optimizations, making it ideal for building iOS apps. To write iOS apps in Swift, developers can create Swift source files (.swift) within their Xcode projects and use Swift syntax to define app logic, data models, user interfaces, and interactions. Swift combines the flexibility and expressiveness of dynamic languages with the safety and performance of compiled languages, enabling developers to write clean, concise, and maintainable code. Xcode provides robust support for Swift development, including syntax highlighting, code completion, error checking, refactoring, and debugging features, to help developers write high-quality code efficiently. In addition to Xcode, Interface Builder, and Swift, iOS app development also involves other tools and technologies such as the iOS Software Development Kit (SDK), Cocoa Touch framework, UIKit framework, Core Data framework, and more. The iOS SDK provides a rich set of APIs and libraries for accessing device hardware, interacting with system services, handling user input, displaying content, and performing other common tasks in iOS apps. The Cocoa Touch framework, built on top of the Foundation framework, provides essential classes and protocols for developing iOS apps, including classes for managing app lifecycle, handling user interface events, and accessing device features. The UIKit framework, a part of the Cocoa Touch framework, provides a collection of classes and protocols for building the user interface of iOS apps, including classes for creating and managing views, view controllers, navigation interfaces, and other UI components. The Core Data framework provides a powerful and efficient mechanism for managing the model layer of iOS apps, enabling developers to define data models, store data locally on the device, and perform complex data operations such as querying, fetching, sorting, and filtering. Overall, mastering the tools and technologies involved in iOS app development, including Xcode, Interface Builder, and Swift, is essential for building high-quality and successful iOS apps that delight users and meet their needs. By leveraging the capabilities of these tools and technologies, developers can create compelling and innovative apps that run seamlessly on Apple's mobile devices and provide a superior user experience.

Creating your first iOS app is an exciting milestone for aspiring developers, marking the beginning of your journey into the world of mobile app development. To embark on this journey, you'll need to familiarize yourself with Xcode, Apple's powerful IDE for building iOS, macOS, watchOS, and tvOS apps. After installing Xcode from the Mac App Store, you can launch it and begin by creating a new Xcode project. From the project template chooser, select the "App" template under the iOS tab, and then choose the "Single View App" template, which is a simple starting point for creating iOS apps. Next, you'll be prompted to enter the product name, organization name, and organization identifier for your app. These details will be used to create the project folder structure and configure your app's bundle identifier. Once you've filled in the necessary information, click "Next" and choose a location to save your project. With the project created, you'll find yourself in the Xcode workspace, where you'll see the project navigator on the left, the editor area in the center, and various utility panes on the right. The project navigator displays the files and folders in your project, while the editor area is where you'll write your code and design your app's user interface. Now, let's start by adding some user interface elements to our app. Open the Main.storyboard file in the project navigator to begin designing your app's interface using Interface Builder. Interface Builder provides a visual canvas where you can drag and drop UI components onto the screen and customize their properties. For our Hello World app, let's keep it simple and add a label to display the greeting message. Drag a Label element from the Object Library onto the view controller's canvas and position it in the center of the screen. Then, resize the label and change its text to "Hello, World!" using the Attributes inspector. With the user interface in place, it's time to connect the label to our code so we can dynamically update its text. To do this, switch to the Assistant Editor view by clicking the "Show the Assistant Editor" button in the Xcode toolbar. This will split the editor area, with the storyboard on one side and the corresponding view controller file on the other. Now, control-click and drag from the label to the view controller file to create an outlet. An outlet is a reference to a UI element in your storyboard that allows you to access and manipulate it programmatically. Give the outlet a name, such as "helloLabel," and then release the mouse button to create the connection. Xcode will generate a property for the outlet in your view controller file, allowing you to refer to the label in your code. Now that we have a reference to the label, let's update its text when the app launches. Switch to the view controller file and find the viewDidLoad() method. This method is called when the view controller's view is loaded into memory, making it a suitable place to initialize the user interface. Inside the viewDidLoad() method, assign the "Hello, World!" string to the text property of the helloLabel outlet. Your code should look like this: swift override func viewDidLoad() { super.viewDidLoad() helloLabel.text = "Hello, World!" } With the code in place, you're ready to run your app in the iOS Simulator to see it in action. In Xcode, select a simulator device from the toolbar, such as iPhone 11, and click the "Run" button. Xcode will build your app, launch the simulator, and install the app on the selected device. After a brief moment, you should see your app's user interface appear in the simulator, with the label displaying the "Hello, World!" message as you specified in code. Congratulations! You've successfully created and run your first iOS app using Xcode. This simple Hello World tutorial provides a foundational understanding of the iOS app development process, introducing you to key concepts such as project setup, user interface design, code editing, and app deployment. As you continue your journey into iOS development, you'll build upon these fundamentals and explore more advanced topics to create increasingly complex and feature-rich apps. With practice, patience, and perseverance, you'll unlock the full potential of the iOS platform and bring your app ideas to life for millions of users around the world.

Chapter 7: Advanced iOS Development Techniques and Tools

Advanced UI/UX design patterns and practices are essential components in creating highly engaging and user-friendly digital experiences. As technology evolves and user expectations continue to rise, designers must stay ahead of the curve by implementing innovative techniques and leveraging best practices to deliver exceptional user interfaces and experiences. One such practice is the implementation of responsive design, which ensures that digital products adapt seamlessly to various screen sizes and devices, providing a consistent user experience across desktops, tablets, and smartphones. To achieve responsive design, designers often utilize CSS media queries to define different layout rules based on the device's screen width, allowing content to reflow and adjust dynamically. Additionally, the use of fluid grids and flexible images helps maintain proportionate layouts and ensures optimal readability and usability across different screen resolutions. Another key aspect of advanced UI/UX design is the incorporation of microinteractions, which are subtle animations and feedback mechanisms that enhance user engagement and delight. Microinteractions can range from simple hover effects and button animations to more complex interactions like swipe gestures and loading animations. By adding these small but meaningful details, designers can create more immersive and interactive experiences that captivate users and encourage deeper engagement with the product. In addition to microinteractions, designers also leverage motion design principles to create fluid transitions and animations that guide users through the interface and communicate important information effectively. Motion design adds depth and dimension to digital products, making them feel more alive and intuitive to navigate. To implement motion design, designers use tools like Adobe After Effects or CSS animations to create smooth transitions between screens, reveal hidden content, and provide visual feedback to user actions. Furthermore, advanced UI/UX design practices involve a deep understanding of user psychology and behavior, allowing designers to anticipate user needs and preferences and tailor the interface accordingly. This includes conducting user research, usability testing, and user persona development to gain insights into user motivations, goals, and pain points. Armed with this knowledge, designers can make informed design decisions and create experiences that resonate with their target audience. Accessibility is another critical consideration in advanced UI/UX design, ensuring that digital products are usable and inclusive for all users, including those with disabilities. Designers follow the Web Content Accessibility Guidelines (WCAG) to ensure that their designs are perceivable, operable, understandable, and robust for users with various disabilities. This involves providing alternative text for images, ensuring proper color contrast for text and background elements, and designing keyboard-friendly navigation for users who rely on assistive technologies. As technology continues to evolve, designers must also adapt their skills and workflows to keep pace with emerging trends and technologies. This includes staying updated on the latest design tools and software, such as Sketch, Figma, and Adobe XD, which streamline the design process and facilitate collaboration among team members. Designers also leverage prototyping tools like InVision and Marvel to create interactive prototypes that simulate the user experience and gather feedback from stakeholders and users early in the design process. Additionally, designers embrace design systems and component libraries to maintain consistency and scalability across their designs, enabling rapid iteration and ensuring a cohesive user experience across all touchpoints. In summary, advanced UI/UX design patterns and practices play a crucial role in shaping the digital landscape and driving user engagement and satisfaction. By incorporating responsive design, microinteractions, motion design, user psychology, accessibility, and emerging technologies into their workflows, designers can create compelling and intuitive experiences that resonate with users and differentiate their products in the competitive marketplace. As technology continues to evolve and user expectations evolve, designers must continue to innovate and push the boundaries of design to deliver exceptional user experiences that delight and inspire.

Utilizing advanced iOS frameworks is essential for developing sophisticated and high-performance iOS applications that meet the demands of modern users. Among these frameworks, Core Data stands out as a powerful and versatile tool for managing the model layer of an application's data. With Core Data, developers can easily define data models, manage object graphs, and persist data to various storage formats such as SQLite databases. To integrate Core Data into an iOS project, developers typically use Xcode's built-in data model editor to define entities, attributes, and relationships, and then generate corresponding managed object subclasses. They can then use Core Data APIs to perform CRUD (Create, Read, Update, Delete) operations on managed objects, fetch data using predicates and sort descriptors, and implement data validation and error handling. Core Data also provides support for concurrency through managed object contexts, allowing developers to perform background data processing tasks without blocking the main thread and affecting the application's responsiveness.

Another essential framework for iOS development is Core Animation, which enables developers to create stunning and interactive user interfaces with smooth animations and transitions. Core Animation leverages the GPU to render animations efficiently, resulting in buttery-smooth performance even on older iOS devices. Developers can use Core Animation to animate UIView properties such as position, size, rotation, and opacity, as well as apply advanced effects like transformations, gradients, and masks. Core Animation also supports keyframe animations, allowing developers to define complex animation sequences with precise timing and interpolation. To incorporate Core Animation into an iOS application, developers typically use UIView's animation APIs or Core Animation's lower-level APIs to create and configure animation objects, specify timing parameters, and add animations to the layer hierarchy.

In addition to Core Data and Core Animation, several other advanced frameworks are available to iOS developers, each serving specific purposes and catering to different aspects of application development. For example, Core Location provides access to the device's GPS and other location services, enabling developers to integrate location-based features such as maps, geocoding, and geofencing into their applications. To utilize Core Location, developers need to request the appropriate permissions from users and configure the desired location accuracy and update frequency. They can then use Core Location APIs to retrieve the device's current location, monitor significant location changes, and perform geospatial calculations.

Another indispensable framework is Core Bluetooth, which enables developers to integrate Bluetooth Low Energy (BLE) connectivity into their iOS applications, allowing them to communicate with external Bluetooth devices such as fitness trackers, smartwatches, and IoT devices. To use Core Bluetooth, developers must first obtain the necessary hardware permissions and enable the appropriate background modes in their application's Info.plist file. They can then use Core Bluetooth APIs to discover nearby BLE peripherals, establish connections, and exchange data using characteristic read, write, and notify operations. Core Bluetooth also provides support for implementing Bluetooth GATT (Generic Attribute Profile) protocols and managing Bluetooth central and peripheral roles.

Furthermore, developers can leverage advanced frameworks like Core ML and Vision to incorporate machine learning and computer vision capabilities into their iOS applications. Core ML allows developers to integrate pre-trained machine learning models into their apps, enabling tasks such as image recognition, natural language processing, and predictive modeling. Vision, on the other hand, provides high-level APIs for performing image analysis and computer vision tasks, including face detection, text recognition, object tracking, and barcode scanning. To utilize Core ML and Vision, developers need to convert their machine learning models into Core ML format using tools like Apple's Core ML Tools or third-party converters. They can then use Core ML

and Vision APIs to load and run the models, process input data, and interpret the results.
Overall, leveraging advanced iOS frameworks is crucial for building modern and feature-rich iOS applications that deliver exceptional user experiences and functionality. By mastering frameworks like Core Data, Core Animation, Core Location, Core Bluetooth, Core ML, and Vision, developers can unlock a wide range of possibilities and create innovative and immersive applications that push the boundaries of what is possible on the iOS platform. With the right combination of frameworks and expertise, developers can build iOS apps that stand out in the App Store and delight users around the world.

Chapter 8: Optimizing iOS Performance and Battery Life

Performance optimization is a critical aspect of software development, especially in the realm of iOS app development, where smooth and responsive user experiences are paramount. To ensure that iOS apps meet performance expectations, developers employ a variety of strategies, including profiling, debugging, and utilizing Instruments.

Profiling involves analyzing the performance of an application to identify bottlenecks and areas for improvement. Xcode, the integrated development environment (IDE) for iOS app development, provides powerful profiling tools that allow developers to measure various aspects of an app's performance, such as CPU usage, memory usage, and network activity. One such tool is the Instruments app, which offers a suite of performance analysis instruments that developers can use to monitor and analyze different aspects of their app's performance in real-time. To launch Instruments from Xcode, developers can use the following CLI command:

bashCopy code

```
$ instruments
```

Once Instruments is running, developers can choose from a variety of instruments, including the Time Profiler, Allocations, and Network instruments, to gather data on different aspects of their app's performance. For example, the Time Profiler instrument provides a detailed view of CPU usage over time, allowing developers to identify hotspots in their code where CPU-intensive operations are occurring. Similarly, the Allocations instrument tracks memory usage and can help identify memory leaks or excessive memory usage by objects in the app.

In addition to profiling, debugging plays a crucial role in performance optimization by allowing developers to identify and fix bugs and issues that may impact performance. Xcode provides robust debugging tools that enable developers to inspect the runtime behavior of their apps, set breakpoints, and step through code to identify and resolve issues. One commonly used debugging technique is symbolic breakpoint debugging, which involves setting breakpoints at specific points in the code where performance issues are suspected to occur. To set a symbolic breakpoint in Xcode, developers can use the following CLI command:

bashCopy code

```
$ breakpoint set -n functionName
```

This command sets a breakpoint at the specified function name, allowing developers to pause execution and inspect the state of the app when the function is called. By strategically placing breakpoints and analyzing the execution flow of their code, developers can pinpoint performance bottlenecks and take corrective action to improve performance.

Moreover, Instruments provides a variety of debugging instruments that developers can use to diagnose and troubleshoot performance issues. For example, the Zombies instrument helps identify memory management issues such as over-released objects or accessing deallocated memory, while the Leaks instrument detects memory leaks by monitoring memory allocations and deallocations over time. By using these instruments in conjunction with profiling tools, developers can gain deep insights into their app's performance characteristics and identify areas for improvement.

Furthermore, developers can utilize advanced techniques such as code optimization and algorithmic improvements to enhance the performance of their iOS apps. This may involve refactoring code to eliminate redundant or inefficient operations, optimizing data structures and algorithms to reduce computational complexity, or adopting best practices for resource management and concurrency. For example, developers can use techniques such as lazy loading, caching, and asynchronous programming to minimize the impact of resource-intensive operations on the main thread and improve overall responsiveness.

Additionally, developers can leverage hardware-accelerated features of iOS devices, such as the Metal framework for high-performance graphics rendering and the Accelerate framework for mathematical and signal processing tasks. By utilizing these frameworks and taking advantage of hardware acceleration capabilities, developers can achieve significant performance improvements in areas such as rendering complex 3D graphics, audio processing, and image manipulation.

In summary, performance optimization is a crucial aspect of iOS app development that requires a combination of profiling, debugging, and strategic optimization techniques. By using profiling tools like Instruments to analyze performance metrics, debugging tools to identify and fix issues, and advanced optimization techniques to improve code efficiency, developers can ensure that their iOS apps deliver exceptional performance and provide users with a smooth and responsive experience.

Battery life optimization is a critical concern for mobile device users, particularly those using iOS devices where power management is paramount. Understanding and implementing techniques to optimize battery life can significantly enhance the user experience. One important aspect of battery life optimization is managing background processing effectively. Background processing refers to the execution of tasks by apps while they are not actively in use or running in the foreground. iOS provides several mechanisms for background processing, such as Background App Refresh and Background Execution Modes, which allow apps to perform tasks such as fetching data, updating content, and responding to notifications even when they are not actively being used by the user. However, excessive background processing can consume significant amounts of battery power, leading to reduced battery life. To mitigate this issue, developers can implement several strategies to minimize background processing and conserve battery power. For example, developers can use background fetch and silent push notifications to schedule periodic updates and downloads when the device is connected to Wi-Fi or charging, rather than continuously polling for updates and consuming battery power. Similarly, developers can leverage background task execution APIs to perform resource-intensive tasks such as data synchronization and content processing in an energy-efficient manner. By prioritizing and optimizing background tasks based on their importance and energy impact, developers can minimize battery drain and improve overall battery life. Another important aspect of battery life optimization is power management. iOS devices employ various power management techniques to optimize battery life and ensure efficient use of power resources. One such technique is CPU throttling, which involves dynamically adjusting the CPU frequency and performance based on system load and resource demands. iOS devices use advanced power management algorithms to intelligently throttle the CPU frequency and voltage to match the processing requirements of running tasks, thereby reducing power consumption and extending battery life. Additionally, iOS devices employ low-power modes such as Low Power Mode and Battery Saver Mode to further conserve battery power during periods of extended use or when the battery level is low. These modes disable non-essential features and background tasks, reduce screen brightness, and optimize system performance to minimize power consumption and prolong battery life. To ensure effective power management, developers can implement best practices for energy-efficient app design and optimize their apps for low-power operation. This may include minimizing CPU and GPU usage, reducing network activity, optimizing UI rendering, and avoiding unnecessary background processing. By following these guidelines and leveraging iOS's built-in power management features, developers can create apps that deliver optimal performance while maximizing battery life. In summary, battery life optimization is a critical aspect of iOS app development, requiring developers to implement strategies for managing background processing and power consumption effectively. By minimizing background processing, prioritizing tasks, and optimizing power management, developers can create apps that deliver superior performance while preserving battery life for a better user experience.

BOOK 5

ANDROID ENGINEERING

MASTERING THE WORLD'S MOST POPULAR MOBILE OS

ROB BOTWRIGHT

Chapter 1: Introduction to Android: History and Architecture

The evolution of Android, from its inception to the present, is a fascinating journey that has transformed the mobile landscape. Android, developed by Android Inc., was founded in 2003 by Andy Rubin, Rich Miner, Nick Sears, and Chris White. In 2005, Google acquired Android Inc., marking the beginning of its journey towards becoming the world's most popular mobile operating system. The first commercial version of Android, Android 1.0, was released in September 2008, introducing features such as the Android Market (now Google Play Store), Google Maps integration, and a web browser based on the WebKit engine. Android 1.5, codenamed Cupcake, followed in April 2009, introducing support for third-party keyboards, widgets, and video recording. With each subsequent release, Android continued to evolve rapidly, introducing new features, enhancements, and improvements to the user experience. Android 2.0, codenamed Eclair, was released in October 2009, bringing significant improvements to the user interface, browser, camera, and contacts applications. Android 2.2, codenamed Froyo, followed in May 2010, introducing features such as support for Adobe Flash, USB tethering, and Wi-Fi hotspot functionality. Android 2.3, codenamed Gingerbread, was released in December 2010, further refining the user interface and introducing features such as Near Field Communication (NFC) support and improved copy and paste functionality. Android 3.0, codenamed Honeycomb, was a major milestone for Android, as it was the first version specifically designed for tablets. Released in February 2011, Honeycomb introduced a redesigned user interface optimized for larger screens, as well as features such as multi-tasking, tabbed browsing, and support for hardware acceleration. Android 4.0, codenamed Ice Cream Sandwich, was released in October 2011, unifying the user interface across smartphones and tablets and introducing features such as facial recognition unlocking, Android Beam for NFC-based sharing, and resizable widgets. Android 4.1, codenamed Jelly Bean, followed in July 2012, introducing features such as Google Now, which provided personalized information and recommendations based on user behavior and preferences. Android 4.4, codenamed KitKat, was released in October 2013, focusing on performance optimization, memory management, and support for lower-end devices. Android 5.0, codenamed Lollipop, was released in November 2014, introducing a new design language called Material Design, which emphasized fluid motion, depth, and intuitive interactions. Lollipop also introduced features such as multiple user accounts, screen pinning, and improved battery life optimization. Android 6.0, codenamed Marshmallow, was released in October 2015, focusing on enhancing the user experience and improving system performance. Marshmallow introduced features such as granular app permissions, Google Now on Tap, and a new power-saving mode called Doze. Android 7.0, codenamed Nougat, was released in August 2016, introducing features such as multi-window support, direct reply notifications, and Vulkan API support for high-performance graphics. Android 8.0, codenamed Oreo, was released in August 2017, focusing on improving system performance, battery life, and security. Oreo introduced features such as background limits for apps, notification channels, and picture-in-picture mode. Android 9.0, codenamed Pie, was released in August 2018, introducing features such as Adaptive Battery, Adaptive Brightness, and Digital Wellbeing tools to help users manage their smartphone usage. Android 10, released in September 2019, focused on privacy and security enhancements, introducing features such as scoped storage, permissions revamp, and a system-wide dark mode. Android 11, released in September 2020, continued to refine the user experience with features such as conversation notifications, bubble notifications, and screen recording. Android 12, released in October 2021, introduced a refreshed design language called Material You, which allowed users to personalize their device experience with custom color schemes, wallpapers, and accents. With each new release, Android continues to evolve and innovate, shaping the future of mobile technology and empowering users with new features, capabilities, and experiences. Understanding the Android architecture is essential for developers and enthusiasts alike to grasp the inner workings of the operating system. At its core, Android is built upon the Linux kernel, which serves as the foundation for the entire system. The Linux kernel provides low-level hardware abstraction, device drivers, memory management, and other essential functionalities required for the operation of the device. Developers can interact with the kernel through various system calls and interfaces, but direct manipulation of the kernel is typically not necessary for application development.

On top of the Linux kernel, Android utilizes a set of libraries that provide additional functionalities and abstractions to developers. These libraries include the C library (libc), which provides standard C functions, as well as other libraries for multimedia processing, graphics rendering, database access, and more. One notable library is the Android Runtime (ART), which is responsible for executing and managing Android applications. ART replaces the earlier Dalvik Virtual Machine (DVM) and uses ahead-of-time (AOT) compilation to improve performance and efficiency.

The Android framework sits above the libraries layer and provides a set of high-level APIs and tools for building applications. This framework consists of various components that developers can leverage to create rich and interactive user experiences. One of the core components of the Android framework is the Activity Manager, which manages the lifecycle of applications and provides a framework for implementing user interfaces. Other essential components include the Content Provider, which allows applications to share data with other applications, and the Notification Manager, which handles notifications and alerts.

At the top of the Android architecture are the applications layer, where user-facing applications reside. These applications are written in Java or Kotlin and run within their own sandboxed environment, isolated from other applications for security and stability purposes. Each application typically consists of one or more activities, services, broadcast receivers, and content providers, which work together to deliver the application's functionality.

To gain insights into the Android architecture and understand how the different layers interact, developers can use various command-line tools and utilities provided by the Android SDK. For example, the adb (Android Debug Bridge) tool allows developers to communicate with an Android device or emulator from a computer and execute various commands, such as installing applications, debugging, and accessing system logs. Additionally, developers can use the pm (Package Manager) command to query information about installed applications, manage packages, and perform other package-related operations.

Understanding the Android architecture is crucial for developers to build efficient and robust applications that leverage the underlying system resources effectively. By understanding the role of each layer in the Android stack, developers can optimize their applications for performance, security, and compatibility across different devices and versions of Android. Additionally, understanding the Android architecture provides developers with insights into how the system works, enabling them to troubleshoot issues, debug problems, and develop innovative solutions that push the boundaries of mobile technology.

Chapter 2: Setting Up Your Development Environment

Installing and configuring Android Studio is a fundamental step for developers looking to build Android applications. Android Studio is the official integrated development environment (IDE) provided by Google for Android app development, offering a comprehensive set of tools and features to streamline the development process. To get started, developers need to download and install Android Studio on their development machine. The installation process varies depending on the operating system, but Google provides straightforward instructions for each platform.

For developers using a Windows machine, the first step is to download the Android Studio installer from the official website. Once the installer is downloaded, it can be executed by double-clicking on the downloaded file. The installer guides users through the installation process, allowing them to choose the installation directory and select additional components to install, such as the Android SDK, Android Virtual Device (AVD) emulator, and additional SDK tools.

On macOS, developers can download the Android Studio.dmg file from the official website and then drag the Android Studio icon into the Applications folder to complete the installation. After the installation is complete, developers can launch Android Studio from the Applications folder and follow the setup wizard to complete the initial configuration.

Linux users can download the Android Studio package in .tar.gz format and extract it to a desired location on their system. Once extracted, developers can navigate to the android-studio/bin directory and launch Android Studio by executing the studio.sh script from the terminal. It's important to ensure that the appropriate permissions are set to execute the script using the chmod command if necessary.

After launching Android Studio for the first time, developers are prompted to download the necessary SDK components and tools required for Android app development. This includes the latest Android SDK platform, build tools, and system images for different Android versions. Developers can choose the components they want to download based on their development needs and target Android versions.

Once the SDK components are downloaded and installed, developers can configure additional settings in Android Studio to customize their development environment. This includes configuring the SDK location, setting up virtual devices for testing using the AVD Manager, and configuring version control integration with Git or other version control systems.

Android Studio provides a rich set of features to enhance productivity and streamline the development workflow. These features include code completion, syntax highlighting, code refactoring tools, and built-in support for debugging and testing. Developers can also take advantage of plugins and extensions to extend the functionality of Android Studio and integrate with other development tools and services.

In addition to the IDE itself, Android Studio also provides access to a wealth of documentation, tutorials, and sample code to help developers learn and master Android app development. The Android Developer website offers comprehensive resources for developers of all skill levels, including guides, API reference documentation, and code samples.

Overall, installing and configuring Android Studio is a crucial first step for developers embarking on Android app development. By setting up a robust development environment with Android Studio, developers can leverage the full power of the

Android platform to build innovative and high-quality mobile applications.

Setting up Android Virtual Devices (AVDs) and physical devices for development is essential for testing and debugging Android applications across different environments. AVDs allow developers to emulate various Android devices and configurations directly on their development machine, while physical devices offer real-world testing scenarios. To create an AVD, developers can use the Android Virtual Device (AVD) Manager, which is integrated into Android Studio. They can access the AVD Manager by navigating to Tools > AVD Manager in the Android Studio menu.

Once in the AVD Manager, developers can create a new virtual device by clicking on the "Create Virtual Device" button. This launches a wizard that guides developers through the process of configuring the virtual device. The wizard prompts developers to choose a hardware profile, which represents the device's specifications such as screen size, resolution, RAM, and CPU architecture. Developers can select from a range of predefined hardware profiles or create custom ones to match specific device configurations.

After selecting a hardware profile, developers need to choose a system image, which represents the Android version and variant (such as Google Play or Android TV) to be installed on the virtual device. System images are downloadable packages provided by Google through the Android SDK Manager. Developers can download and install system images for different Android versions and variants directly from the Android Studio SDK Manager.

Once the system image is selected, developers can configure additional settings such as the device name, orientation, and scale factor. They can also specify advanced settings such as camera support, hardware acceleration, and emulator performance options. Once all the settings are configured, developers can click on the "Finish" button to create the virtual device.

Once the virtual device is created, developers can launch it by selecting it from the AVD Manager and clicking on the "Play" button. This launches the Android Emulator, which starts the virtual device and boots it into the selected Android system image. Developers can interact with the virtual device using the emulator controls, which simulate touch input, hardware buttons, and sensor input.

In addition to virtual devices, developers can also test their applications on physical Android devices. To do this, developers need to enable developer mode and USB debugging on their Android device. This involves accessing the device's settings, navigating to the "About phone" or "About tablet" section, and tapping on the "Build number" multiple times until developer mode is enabled. Once developer mode is enabled, developers can access the developer options menu in the device settings and enable USB debugging.

Once USB debugging is enabled, developers can connect their Android device to their development machine using a USB cable. The first time the device is connected, developers may need to authorize the connection on the device itself. Once authorized, the device appears in the list of connected devices in Android Studio's Device File Explorer and can be used for debugging and testing.

Both AVDs and physical devices offer unique advantages for Android development. AVDs provide a convenient way to test applications across different device configurations and Android versions without the need for physical hardware. However, they may not accurately reflect the performance and behavior of real devices. On the other hand, testing on physical devices offers a more realistic testing environment but may require additional setup and maintenance.

Overall, setting up Android Virtual Devices (AVDs) and physical devices for development is a critical step in the Android app development process. By leveraging both virtual and physical testing environments, developers can ensure that their applications work seamlessly across a wide range of devices and configurations, leading to a better user experience for their users.

Chapter 3: Exploring the Android Studio IDE

Navigating the Android Studio interface is essential for efficient development and management of Android projects. Android Studio provides a comprehensive set of tools and features to streamline the app development process, and understanding how to navigate its interface is crucial for developers. Upon launching Android Studio, developers are greeted with a workspace that consists of several key components, including the toolbar, editor window, project explorer, and various tool windows.

The toolbar at the top of the Android Studio window contains essential actions and controls for managing projects and executing commands. It includes buttons for building and running projects, syncing with version control systems, and accessing various tools and settings. The toolbar also provides quick access to device and emulator configurations for testing applications.

The editor window is where developers write and edit code, XML layouts, and other project files. Android Studio supports syntax highlighting, code completion, and code navigation features to help developers write code more efficiently.

Developers can switch between different files and tabs using keyboard shortcuts or by clicking on the corresponding tabs in the editor window.

The project explorer, located on the left side of the Android Studio window, displays the project structure and files in a hierarchical view. It allows developers to navigate through the project's directories, view file contents, and perform file management tasks. Developers can expand and collapse directories, search for files, and organize files into groups using the project explorer.

Android Studio also includes various tool windows that provide additional functionality and tools for development. These tool windows can be accessed from the View menu or by using keyboard shortcuts. Some of the most commonly used tool windows include the Android Profiler, Logcat, and Device File Explorer, which help developers monitor app performance, view log messages, and explore device files, respectively.

The Android Profiler tool window provides real-time performance monitoring and profiling capabilities for Android applications. It allows developers to monitor CPU, memory, and network usage, as well as analyze app behavior and performance bottlenecks. Developers can use the Android Profiler to identify performance issues and optimize their applications for better performance.

The Logcat tool window displays log messages generated by the Android system and applications running on the device or emulator. It provides developers with valuable information about app behavior, errors, warnings, and debug messages, helping them diagnose and troubleshoot issues during development. Developers can filter and search log messages, as well as customize logcat output to focus on specific types of messages.

The Device File Explorer tool window enables developers to browse and manage files on connected Android devices and emulators. It allows developers to view file contents, copy files between the device and the development machine, and perform various file management tasks. Developers can use the Device File Explorer to inspect app data, transfer files, and debug file-related issues.

In addition to these tool windows, Android Studio also includes a range of other tools and features to support Android development, such as the Layout Editor, Resource Manager, and Database Inspector. These tools provide developers with powerful capabilities for designing user interfaces, managing project resources, and debugging database interactions.

Overall, navigating the Android Studio interface is a fundamental skill for Android developers. By familiarizing themselves with the various components and tools available in Android Studio, developers can work more efficiently, write better code, and build high-quality Android applications.

Utilizing key features and tools in Android Studio is essential for efficient and effective Android app development. Android Studio provides a wide range of features and tools that enable developers to streamline their workflow, improve productivity, and build high-quality applications. One of the key features of Android Studio is its intelligent code editor, which offers advanced code completion, syntax highlighting, and code navigation capabilities. Developers can leverage these features to write code faster, identify errors, and navigate through their codebase with ease.

The code editor also includes powerful refactoring tools that allow developers to rename variables, extract methods, and optimize code structure with minimal effort. By using these refactoring tools, developers can improve code readability, maintainability, and overall code quality. Additionally, Android Studio supports code templates and snippets, enabling developers to

insert commonly used code patterns and accelerate development tasks.
Another key feature of Android Studio is its built-in emulator, which allows developers to test their applications on a variety of virtual devices with different screen sizes, resolutions, and Android versions. Developers can launch the emulator directly from Android Studio and deploy their apps for testing without needing physical devices. The emulator provides various debugging and testing capabilities, such as simulating device sensors, capturing screenshots, and recording video of app interactions.
For real-time testing and debugging, Android Studio offers seamless integration with physical Android devices. Developers can connect their devices to their development machine via USB or Wi-Fi and deploy their apps directly to the device for testing. Android Studio automatically detects connected devices and allows developers to run and debug their apps on them with ease. This feature is particularly useful for testing apps on real hardware and ensuring compatibility across different devices.
Android Studio also includes a comprehensive set of profiling tools that help developers analyze app performance, identify performance bottlenecks, and optimize resource usage. The Android Profiler

tool provides real-time monitoring of CPU, memory, and network usage, as well as detailed insights into app behavior and performance metrics. Developers can use the Android Profiler to detect performance issues, optimize code, and improve app responsiveness and efficiency.

In addition to performance profiling, Android Studio includes tools for debugging and analyzing app behavior. The Logcat tool allows developers to view log messages generated by their app and the Android system, helping them diagnose and troubleshoot issues during development. Developers can filter log messages, search for specific messages, and customize logcat output to focus on relevant information.

Android Studio also offers powerful layout and resource management tools that simplify the process of designing user interfaces and managing project resources. The Layout Editor allows developers to visually design UI layouts, drag and drop UI components, and preview UI designs in real-time. The Resource Manager provides a centralized location for managing app resources, such as images, strings, and layouts, and allows developers to organize and access resources efficiently.

Furthermore, Android Studio includes built-in support for version control systems, such as Git,

enabling developers to manage and collaborate on their projects effectively. Developers can clone, commit, push, and pull changes directly from Android Studio, as well as resolve merge conflicts and view revision history. This integration simplifies the process of version control and facilitates team collaboration on Android projects.
Overall, Android Studio offers a rich set of features and tools that empower developers to create high-quality Android applications efficiently. By leveraging these key features and tools, developers can streamline their workflow, improve productivity, and deliver polished and performant apps to users.

Chapter 4: Understanding Android App Components: Activities, Services, and Broadcast Receivers

Exploring the different components of an Android app provides a comprehensive understanding of its architecture and functionality. Android apps are composed of various components, each serving a specific purpose in the app lifecycle and user interaction. One of the fundamental components of an Android app is the activity, which represents a single screen with a user interface. Activities are the building blocks of the app's UI and are responsible for handling user interactions, such as button clicks, gestures, and text input. Developers can create activities by extending the Activity class and defining UI layout using XML or programmatically.

In addition to activities, Android apps may also contain fragments, which are reusable UI components that can be combined to create flexible and dynamic user interfaces. Fragments allow developers to modularize UI components and adapt the app's layout to different screen sizes and orientations. Like activities, fragments have their lifecycle and can be added, removed, or replaced dynamically within an activity's layout.

Another essential component of an Android app is the service, which runs in the background to perform long-running operations or handle tasks that do not require user interaction. Services are commonly used for tasks such as playing music, downloading files, or syncing data with a remote server. Developers can create services by extending the Service class and implementing the desired functionality within the service's onStartCommand() method.

Broadcast receivers are another key component of Android apps, responsible for receiving and handling system-wide broadcast messages or custom events. Broadcast receivers allow apps to respond to system events, such as device boot, network connectivity changes, or incoming SMS messages. Developers can register broadcast receivers either statically in the app's manifest file or dynamically at runtime using the registerReceiver() method.

Content providers are yet another important component of Android apps, responsible for managing and sharing app data with other apps or system components. Content providers encapsulate access to structured data, such as databases or files, and allow other apps to query, insert, update, or delete data through a content URI. Content providers facilitate data sharing and enable apps to interact with each other in a secure and controlled manner.

Lastly, Android manifest file acts as a central configuration file for an Android app, containing essential information about the app's components, permissions, and metadata. The manifest file declares all the activities, services, broadcast receivers, and content providers that comprise the app, as well as any required permissions or hardware features. Developers can also specify app metadata, such as the app's name, version, and icon, in the manifest file.

Overall, exploring the different components of an Android app provides developers with a deeper insight into its architecture and functionality. By understanding the roles and responsibilities of each component, developers can design more robust and efficient apps that meet the needs of users and deliver a seamless user experience.

Understanding the lifecycles and interactions of activities, services, and broadcast receivers is crucial for developing robust and efficient Android applications. Each of these components plays a vital role in the overall functionality and user experience of an app, and knowing how they interact with each other is essential for proper app behavior.

Activities, as mentioned earlier, represent the UI and user interaction of an Android application. They have a lifecycle consisting of several states, including onCreate(), onStart(), onResume(), onPause(), onStop(), and onDestroy(). These lifecycle methods are called at different points in an activity's existence, allowing developers to manage resources, handle user input, and save or restore state data as needed.

Understanding the activity lifecycle is essential for managing resources efficiently and ensuring a smooth user experience. For example, developers can release resources in the onStop() method to free up memory when an activity is no longer visible to the user. They can also save and restore instance state data in the onSaveInstanceState() and onRestoreInstanceState() methods to preserve the app's state across configuration changes, such as screen rotations.

Services, on the other hand, are background tasks that can perform long-running operations without requiring user interaction. Unlike activities, services do not have a UI and typically run in the background to perform tasks such as playing music, downloading files, or syncing data. Services have a simpler lifecycle compared to activities, consisting of only two states: started and stopped. To create a service, developers typically create a subclass of the Service class and implement the desired functionality in the onStartCommand() method. They can then start the service using the startService() method or bind to it using the bindService() method. Services continue to run in the background even if the app's activities are destroyed or the app is no longer in the foreground, making them ideal for tasks that need to continue running indefinitely.

Broadcast receivers are components that respond to system-wide broadcast messages or custom events. They allow apps to receive notifications about system events, such as device boot, network connectivity changes, or incoming SMS messages, and perform actions in response. Broadcast receivers have a lifecycle that is tied to the lifecycle of the application's process, and they are typically registered either statically in the app's manifest file or dynamically at runtime.

To create a broadcast receiver, developers typically create a subclass of the BroadcastReceiver class and override the onReceive() method to handle incoming broadcast messages. They can then register the receiver using either a <receiver> element in the manifest file or the registerReceiver() method at runtime. Broadcast receivers are useful for responding to events that occur outside the app's scope and can be used to trigger actions or start services in response to system events.

Understanding how activities, services, and broadcast receivers interact with each other is crucial for building complex and responsive Android applications. Activities are responsible for presenting the UI to the user and handling user interaction, while services handle background tasks that require no user interaction. Broadcast receivers allow apps to respond to system events and perform actions even when the app is not actively running. By mastering the lifecycles and interactions of these components, developers can create powerful and seamless Android applications that meet the needs of users and deliver a great user experience.

Chapter 5: Working with User Interface Elements: Views and Layouts

Understanding Views and ViewGroups is fundamental to Android app development as they form the building blocks of the user interface. In Android, a View represents a single UI element, such as a button, text field, or image, while a ViewGroup is a special type of View that can contain other Views. By mastering these concepts, developers can create dynamic and responsive user interfaces that enhance the user experience.

Views are the basic building blocks of any Android user interface. They represent the visual elements that users interact with, such as buttons, text fields, checkboxes, and images. Each View is a subclass of the android.view.View class and is responsible for drawing itself on the screen and responding to user input events.

To create a View in Android, developers can either define it in XML layout files or create it programmatically in Java or Kotlin code. In XML layout files, Views are defined using XML tags, such as <Button>, <TextView>, <ImageView>, etc. Developers can specify various attributes, such as size, position, appearance, and behavior, using

XML attributes. For example, to create a button with a specific text label, developers can use the android:text attribute:

xmlCopy code

```
<Button android:id="@+id/myButton"
android:layout_width="wrap_content"
android:layout_height="wrap_content"
android:text="Click Me" />
```

Alternatively, developers can create Views programmatically in Java or Kotlin code using the appropriate constructors and setter methods. For example, to create a Button programmatically, developers can use the Button class constructor and set its text label using the setText() method:

javaCopy code

```
Button myButton = new Button(context);
myButton.setLayoutParams(new
ViewGroup.LayoutParams(
ViewGroup.LayoutParams.WRAP_CONTENT,
ViewGroup.LayoutParams.WRAP_CONTENT));
myButton.setText("Click Me");
```

Once created, Views can be added to a ViewGroup to form the user interface hierarchy. ViewGroup is a subclass of View that provides layout support for organizing multiple Views on the screen. Examples of ViewGroup subclasses include LinearLayout, RelativeLayout, FrameLayout, ConstraintLayout, and others.

Layout managers, such as LinearLayout and RelativeLayout, determine the position and size of child Views within a ViewGroup based on layout rules specified in XML or programmatically. For example, a LinearLayout arranges child Views in either a horizontal or vertical orientation, while a RelativeLayout allows developers to position child Views relative to each other or to the parent ViewGroup.

To add Views to a ViewGroup in XML layout files, developers can use nested XML tags to define the hierarchy. For example, to create a LinearLayout with two TextViews stacked vertically, developers can use the following XML code:

xmlCopy code

```
<LinearLayout
android:layout_width="match_parent"
android:layout_height="match_parent"
android:orientation="vertical">             <TextView
android:id="@+id/textView1"
android:layout_width="wrap_content"
android:layout_height="wrap_content"
android:text="Hello,   World!"   />   <TextView
android:id="@+id/textView2"
android:layout_width="wrap_content"
android:layout_height="wrap_content"
android:text="Welcome          to          Android
Development!" /> </LinearLayout>
```

In addition to adding Views to a ViewGroup statically in XML layout files, developers can also add Views dynamically at runtime in Java or Kotlin code. This allows for more flexibility and customization, as Views can be created, modified, and removed programmatically based on application logic and user interaction.

For example, to add a TextView dynamically to a LinearLayout at runtime, developers can use the addView() method:

javaCopy code

```
LinearLayout layout = findViewById(R.id.myLinearLayout); TextView textView = new TextView(context); textView.setLayoutParams(new ViewGroup.LayoutParams( ViewGroup.LayoutParams.WRAP_CONTENT, ViewGroup.LayoutParams.WRAP_CONTENT)); textView.setText("Dynamic TextView"); layout.addView(textView);
```

Understanding Views and ViewGroups is essential for creating dynamic and responsive user interfaces in Android. By mastering these concepts, developers can design visually appealing layouts that adapt to different screen sizes and orientations and provide an intuitive user experience. Whether defining Views in XML layout files or creating them programmatically, developers have the flexibility to create rich and interactive user interfaces that meet the requirements of their Android applications.

Creating user interfaces in Android involves utilizing various layout managers to organize and position UI elements effectively. Among the most commonly used layout managers are LinearLayout, RelativeLayout, and ConstraintLayout, each offering unique features and flexibility in designing Android UIs.

LinearLayout is a simple layout manager that arranges its child views either horizontally or vertically. It is ideal for creating straightforward UI designs where views are aligned in a single row or column. The orientation of a LinearLayout can be set to either horizontal or vertical, allowing developers to control the layout direction based on the desired design.

To create a LinearLayout in XML, developers use the <LinearLayout> tag and specify the orientation attribute as either "horizontal" or "vertical." For example:

xmlCopy code

```
<LinearLayout
android:layout_width="match_parent"
android:layout_height="wrap_content"
```

```
android:orientation="vertical"> <!-- Child views go
here --> </LinearLayout>
```

RelativeLayout, on the other hand, is a more flexible layout manager that allows developers to position views relative to each other or to the parent layout. Views within a RelativeLayout can be aligned relative to the parent layout's edges, each other, or specific guidelines. This provides greater control over the placement of UI elements and enables complex UI designs.

To use RelativeLayout in XML, developers define views and their positioning using various layout attributes such as layout_alignParentTop, layout_alignParentBottom, layout_toStartOf, layout_above, etc. For example:

xmlCopy code

```
<RelativeLayout
android:layout_width="match_parent"
android:layout_height="match_parent">
<TextView android:id="@+id/textView1"
android:layout_width="wrap_content"
android:layout_height="wrap_content"
android:text="Hello, World!"
android:layout_alignParentTop="true"
android:layout_centerHorizontal="true"/>
<Button android:id="@+id/button1"
android:layout_width="wrap_content"
android:layout_height="wrap_content"
```

```
android:text="Click Me"
android:layout_below="@id/textView1"
android:layout_centerHorizontal="true"/>
</RelativeLayout>
```

ConstraintLayout is a powerful layout manager introduced in Android Studio that allows developers to create complex UIs with flexible constraints between views. It offers a flat view hierarchy and superior performance compared to nested layouts like LinearLayout and RelativeLayout. ConstraintLayout is particularly useful for designing responsive UIs that adapt to various screen sizes and orientations.

To use ConstraintLayout, developers define constraints between views to specify their relative positioning and sizing. Constraints can be set to the parent layout's edges or to other views, providing precise control over the layout. ConstraintLayout also offers features such as chains, guidelines, and barriers for advanced layout scenarios.

xmlCopy code

```
<androidx.constraintlayout.widget.ConstraintLayo
ut android:layout_width="match_parent"
android:layout_height="match_parent">
<TextView android:id="@+id/textView1"
android:layout_width="wrap_content"
android:layout_height="wrap_content"
```

```
android:text="Hello, World!"
app:layout_constraintTop_toTopOf="parent"
app:layout_constraintStart_toStartOf="parent"
app:layout_constraintEnd_toEndOf="parent"/>
<Button android:id="@+id/button1"
android:layout_width="wrap_content"
android:layout_height="wrap_content"
android:text="Click Me"
app:layout_constraintTop_toBottomOf="@id/text
View1"
app:layout_constraintStart_toStartOf="parent"
app:layout_constraintEnd_toEndOf="parent"/>
</androidx.constraintlayout.widget.ConstraintLay
out>
```

In addition to LinearLayout, RelativeLayout, and ConstraintLayout, Android also provides other layout managers such as FrameLayout, GridLayout, TableLayout, and CoordinatorLayout, each catering to specific layout requirements. By leveraging these layout managers effectively, developers can create visually appealing and responsive user interfaces for their Android applications.

Chapter 6: Managing Data Persistence: SQLite and Content Providers

SQLite is a lightweight, self-contained, serverless, and open-source relational database management system that is embedded directly into Android devices, making it an integral part of Android app development. It provides a simple and efficient way to store and manage structured data within Android applications. SQLite databases are widely used in Android development for various purposes, such as storing user data, application settings, cached data, and more. To begin working with SQLite databases in Android, developers first need to understand the basic concepts and components of SQLite databases. A SQLite database consists of one or more tables, each of which contains rows and columns of data. Tables are defined with a schema that specifies the structure of the data, including the names and data types of the columns. Data is stored in rows within these tables, with each row representing a single record or entry.

In Android development, SQLite databases are typically created and managed using the SQLiteOpenHelper class, which provides methods for creating, opening, upgrading, and managing SQLite databases. Developers can subclass SQLiteOpenHelper and override its onCreate() and onUpgrade() methods to define the database schema and perform any necessary database migrations or upgrades.

To create a new SQLite database in an Android application, developers can create a subclass of SQLiteOpenHelper and override its onCreate() method to define the database schema. They can then call the getWritableDatabase() or getReadableDatabase() method of the SQLiteOpenHelper class to get a reference to the database and perform read and write operations.

javaCopy code

```
public class MyDatabaseHelper extends SQLiteOpenHelper { private static final String DATABASE_NAME = "my_database.db"; private static final int DATABASE_VERSION = 1; public MyDatabaseHelper(Context context) { super(context, DATABASE_NAME, null, DATABASE_VERSION); } @Override public void onCreate(SQLiteDatabase db) { // Create tables and define schema String createTableQuery = "CREATE TABLE IF NOT EXISTS my_table (" + "_id INTEGER PRIMARY KEY AUTOINCREMENT," + "name TEXT," + "age INTEGER)"; db.execSQL(createTableQuery); } @Override
```

public void onUpgrade(SQLiteDatabase db, int oldVersion, int newVersion) { // Perform database upgrade or migration db.execSQL("DROP TABLE IF EXISTS my_table"); onCreate(db); } }

Once the SQLite database is created, developers can use SQL commands to perform various operations such as inserting, updating, deleting, and querying data. SQLite provides a rich set of SQL commands for manipulating data, including SELECT, INSERT, UPDATE, DELETE, and more.

To insert data into a SQLite database in Android, developers can use the SQLiteDatabase class's insert() method, passing in the table name and a ContentValues object containing the data to be inserted. Similarly, to query data from a SQLite database, developers can use the query() method of the SQLiteDatabase class, passing in the table name, columns to retrieve, selection criteria, and other parameters.

javaCopy code

// Inserting data into the database ContentValues values = new ContentValues(); values.put("name", "John"); values.put("age", 30); long rowId = db.insert("my_table", null, values); // Querying data from the database String[] projection = {"_id", "name", "age"}; String selection = "age > ?"; String[] selectionArgs = {"25"}; Cursor cursor =

```
db.query("my_table", projection, selection, selectionArgs, null, null, null);
```

SQLite databases in Android are stored locally on the device's file system and are private to the application that creates them. They are typically stored in the /data/data/package_name/databases directory of the device's internal storage. Developers can use the Android Device Monitor or adb shell commands to access and inspect the SQLite databases stored on a device.

bashCopy code

```
adb shell cd /data/data/package_name/databases
ls
```

In addition to basic CRUD (Create, Read, Update, Delete) operations, SQLite databases in Android support advanced features such as transactions, indexing, and querying with complex SQL statements. Transactions allow developers to group multiple database operations into a single atomic unit, ensuring data integrity and consistency. Indexing can improve the performance of database queries by creating indexes on frequently queried columns.

SQLite databases are an essential component of Android app development, providing a lightweight and efficient way to store and manage structured data within Android applications. By leveraging the power and flexibility of SQLite, developers can create robust and scalable Android apps that effectively manage and persist data to meet the needs of users. Content Providers are a fundamental component of the Android framework, facilitating data access and sharing among different applications installed on the device. They serve as an abstraction layer that allows applications to securely access and manipulate data stored in various data sources, such as databases, files, and network resources. Content Providers follow the ContentProvider class, which defines a standard interface for interacting with data.

In Android, Content Providers are typically used to expose structured data to other applications, enabling them to perform CRUD (Create, Read, Update, Delete) operations on the underlying data source. This data can include anything from contact information and media files to application settings and user preferences. Content Providers play a crucial role in promoting data isolation and security by enforcing permissions and access controls on the shared data.

Developers can create custom Content Providers to expose data from their applications to other applications on the device. To implement a Content Provider in Android, developers need to define a subclass of the ContentProvider class and override several key methods to handle data access requests. These methods include onCreate(), query(), insert(), update(), delete(), getType(), and others.

javaCopy code

public class MyContentProvider extends ContentProvider { // Define content provider constants private static final String AUTHORITY = "com.example.myapp.provider"; private static final String TABLE_NAME = "my_table"; private static final int URI_CODE = 1; private static final UriMatcher uriMatcher = new UriMatcher(UriMatcher.NO_MATCH); static { uriMatcher.addURI(AUTHORITY, TABLE_NAME, URI_CODE); } // Implement content provider methods @Override public boolean onCreate() { // Initialize content provider return true; } @Nullable @Override public Cursor query(@NonNull Uri uri, @Nullable String[] projection, @Nullable String selection, @Nullable String[] selectionArgs, @Nullable String sortOrder) { // Perform query operation SQLiteDatabase db = dbHelper.getReadableDatabase(); Cursor cursor = db.query(TABLE_NAME, projection, selection, selectionArgs, null, null, sortOrder); return cursor; } @Nullable @Override public Uri insert(@NonNull Uri uri, @Nullable ContentValues

values) { // Perform insert operation } @Override public int update(@NonNull Uri uri, @Nullable ContentValues values, @Nullable String selection, @Nullable String[] selectionArgs) { // Perform update operation } @Override public int delete(@NonNull Uri uri, @Nullable String selection, @Nullable String[] selectionArgs) { // Perform delete operation } @Nullable @Override public String getType(@NonNull Uri uri) { // Return MIME type of data } }

Once the Content Provider is implemented, developers need to register it in the AndroidManifest.xml file to declare its presence and define the authority under which it will be accessed. They also need to specify the permissions required to access the Content Provider, including read and write permissions if applicable.

xmlCopy code

```
<provider android:name=".MyContentProvider" android:authorities="com.example.myapp.provider" android:exported="true" android:readPermission="com.example.myapp.permission.READ_PROVIDER" android:writePermission="com.example.myapp.permission.WRITE_PROVIDER" />
```

To access data from a Content Provider in another application, developers need to use a

ContentResolver object to send queries and commands to the Content Provider. They use the URI of the Content Provider along with appropriate query parameters to specify the data they want to access. ContentResolver provides methods like query(), insert(), update(), and delete() to perform these operations. javaCopy code Uri uri = Uri.parse("content://com.example.myapp.provider/my_table"); Cursor cursor = getContentResolver().query(uri, null, null, null, null);

Content Providers in Android support various URI patterns, allowing developers to expose different subsets of data and define granular permissions for accessing them. Additionally, they can implement custom MIME types to specify the type of data returned by the Content Provider, enabling clients to handle data in a standardized manner.

Overall, Content Providers play a crucial role in enabling data sharing and interoperability between Android applications. By implementing Content Providers effectively, developers can create robust and secure applications that leverage the power of data sharing to enhance user experience and functionality.

Chapter 7: Mastering Background Processing and Multithreading

Implementing background tasks is a crucial aspect of Android development, allowing developers to perform long-running operations without blocking the user interface (UI) thread. Two common approaches for implementing background tasks in Android are AsyncTask and Thread.

AsyncTask is a utility class provided by the Android framework that enables developers to perform asynchronous operations on a separate thread and update the UI thread with the results. AsyncTask simplifies the process of managing background tasks by handling thread creation, execution, and completion callbacks internally. However, AsyncTask is suitable for short-lived tasks and may not be suitable for long-running operations due to its limitations.

To use AsyncTask in an Android application, developers need to subclass the AsyncTask class and implement the doInBackground() method to execute the background task. They can also override other methods such as onPreExecute(), onPostExecute(), onProgressUpdate(), and onCancelled() to handle various stages of the task lifecycle.

javaCopy code

```
public class MyAsyncTask extends AsyncTask<Void, Void, String> { @Override protected void onPreExecute() { // Perform setup tasks before executing background task } @Override protected String doInBackground(Void... voids) { // Perform background task return "Task completed"; } @Override protected void onPostExecute(String result) { // Handle UI updates after task completion } }
```

Once the AsyncTask subclass is defined, developers can create an instance of the AsyncTask and execute it using the execute() method. The doInBackground() method will be executed on a background thread, while the onPostExecute() method will be called on the UI thread after the task completes.

javaCopy code

```
MyAsyncTask task = new MyAsyncTask(); task.execute();
```

While AsyncTask provides a convenient way to perform background tasks, it has some limitations, such as difficulty in managing multiple asynchronous operations simultaneously and potential memory leaks if not used properly. In cases where more control over thread management is required, developers can use the Thread class directly.

Thread is a fundamental class in Java that represents a separate thread of execution. Unlike AsyncTask, Thread provides more flexibility and control over the execution of background tasks. Developers can create a new Thread object and pass a Runnable implementation to its constructor to define the code that will run on the background thread.

javaCopy code

```
Thread thread = new Thread(new Runnable() { @Override public void run() { // Perform background task } }); thread.start();
```

Using Thread directly allows developers to manage thread lifecycle, handle exceptions, and implement custom thread pooling mechanisms. However, it requires more boilerplate code compared to AsyncTask and may be less suitable for simple background tasks.

In addition to AsyncTask and Thread, developers can also use other concurrency mechanisms provided by the Java concurrency framework, such as Executor, ThreadPoolExecutor, and FutureTask, to implement background tasks in Android applications. These classes offer more advanced features for managing concurrency and parallelism in multi-threaded environments.

Overall, implementing background tasks using AsyncTask and Thread is essential for building responsive and efficient Android applications. Developers should choose the appropriate approach based on the requirements of the task, considering factors such as simplicity, performance, and resource management. By effectively managing background tasks, developers can create smoother user experiences and avoid UI freezes or application crashes caused by blocking the main UI thread.

Utilizing Android's multithreading frameworks is essential for developing responsive and efficient applications that can perform tasks concurrently without blocking the main UI thread. Android provides several built-in mechanisms for multithreading, including Handlers, Loaders, and Executors, each serving different purposes and offering distinct advantages.

Handlers are a fundamental component of Android's messaging system, allowing communication between different threads. They are commonly used to schedule tasks to be executed on the main UI thread or to send messages and Runnable objects to be processed by Handler threads. Developers can create a Handler associated with the main UI thread by instantiating it in the UI thread's context.

javaCopy code

```
Handler handler = new Handler(Looper.getMainLooper());
```

Once created, developers can post Runnable objects to the Handler's message queue using the post() method. These Runnables will be executed sequentially on the UI thread, ensuring UI updates are performed safely.

javaCopy code

```
handler.post(new Runnable() { @Override public void run() { // Perform UI update } });
```

Handlers are particularly useful for updating the UI from background threads or performing periodic tasks on the main thread, such as updating UI elements in response to user interactions or network events.

Loaders are a part of Android's framework for loading data asynchronously, typically from a content provider or a data source. They are designed to simplify the process of loading data in an activity or fragment while managing the lifecycle and configuration changes automatically. Loaders run on separate threads from the UI thread and deliver results asynchronously to the calling component.

To use a Loader in an Android application, developers typically implement a LoaderManager.LoaderCallbacks interface in their activity or fragment and override the onCreateLoader(), onLoadFinished(), and onLoaderReset() methods to manage the loader's lifecycle and data loading process.

javaCopy code

```
public class MyActivity extends AppCompatActivity
implements LoaderManager.LoaderCallbacks<String>
{ @Override protected void onCreate(Bundle
savedInstanceState) {
super.onCreate(savedInstanceState);
setContentView(R.layout.activity_main); // Initialize
loader getSupportLoaderManager().initLoader(0, null,
this); } @NonNull @Override public Loader<String>
onCreateLoader(int id, @Nullable Bundle args) { //
Create and return a new Loader instance return new
MyLoader(this); } @Override public void
onLoadFinished(@NonNull Loader<String> loader,
```

String data) { // Handle the loaded data } @Override public void onLoaderReset(@NonNull Loader<String> loader) { // Reset loader state } }

Loaders offer automatic data reloading on configuration changes, such as screen rotations, and handle complex data loading scenarios efficiently, making them suitable for tasks like loading large datasets or accessing content providers.

Executors are part of Java's concurrency framework and provide a high-level API for managing concurrent tasks in Android applications. Executors simplify the process of creating and managing threads by providing thread pooling and task scheduling capabilities.

Developers can create an Executor instance using one of the static factory methods available in the Executors class, such as newSingleThreadExecutor(), newFixedThreadPool(), or newCachedThreadPool(), depending on their requirements.

javaCopy code

```
Executor executor = Executors.newSingleThreadExecutor();
```

Once created, developers can submit Runnable or Callable tasks to the Executor for execution using the execute() or submit() methods.

javaCopy code

```
executor.execute(new Runnable() { @Override public void run() { // Perform background task } });
```

Executors abstract away the complexities of managing threads and provide a flexible and efficient way to execute tasks concurrently. They are suitable for scenarios where fine-grained control over thread management is required or when implementing complex concurrency patterns like producer-consumer or parallel processing.

In summary, Android's multithreading frameworks, including Handlers, Loaders, and Executors, offer developers powerful tools for implementing concurrent processing and improving application responsiveness. By understanding the strengths and use cases of each framework, developers can choose the appropriate approach for their specific requirements and build high-performance Android applications.

Chapter 8: Advanced Topics in Android Development: Security, Performance, and Optimization

Securing Android apps is paramount to protect sensitive user data and maintain the integrity of the application. Several best practices and techniques can be employed to enhance the security of Android apps, including data encryption, permission management, and adopting secure coding practices.

One fundamental aspect of securing Android apps is data encryption. Encrypting sensitive data stored on the device helps prevent unauthorized access, even if the device is compromised. Android provides various APIs and libraries for implementing data encryption, such as the Android Keystore system and the Java Cryptography Architecture (JCA).

The Android Keystore system allows developers to store cryptographic keys securely in hardware-backed storage areas, such as Trusted Execution Environments (TEEs) or Secure Elements (SEs). These keys can be used to encrypt and decrypt sensitive data within the app, ensuring that the data remains protected, even if the device is rooted or compromised.

To utilize the Android Keystore system for data encryption, developers can generate cryptographic keys using the KeyGenParameterSpec class and store them securely in the keystore. They can then use these keys to perform encryption and decryption operations using cryptographic algorithms such as AES (Advanced Encryption Standard).

javaCopy code

```
KeyGenerator keyGenerator = KeyGenerator.getInstance(KeyProperties.KEY_ALGORITHM_AES, "AndroidKeyStore"); KeyGenParameterSpec.Builder builder = new KeyGenParameterSpec.Builder("myKeyAlias", KeyProperties.PURPOSE_ENCRYPT | KeyProperties.PURPOSE_DECRYPT)
.setBlockModes(KeyProperties.BLOCK_MODE_CBC)
.setEncryptionPaddings(KeyProperties.ENCRYPTION_PADDING_PKCS7)
.setRandomizedEncryptionRequired(false);
keyGenerator.init(builder.build()); SecretKey secretKey = keyGenerator.generateKey();
```

Once the cryptographic key is generated and stored securely in the keystore, developers can use it to create a Cipher object for encryption and decryption.

javaCopy code

```
Cipher cipher = Cipher.getInstance("AES/CBC/PKCS7Padding");
cipher.init(Cipher.ENCRYPT_MODE, secretKey);
byte[] encryptedData = cipher.doFinal(plainText.getBytes());
```

Another crucial aspect of Android app security is managing permissions effectively. Android's permission model allows users to control which resources and data an app can access on their devices. It's essential for developers to request only the permissions necessary for the app's functionality and to explain to users why each permission is required.

Developers should carefully review and minimize the permissions requested by their apps to reduce the risk of potential misuse or data leakage. Additionally, they should regularly review and update their app's permission requests to align with changes in the app's features and functionality.

xmlCopy code

```xml
<manifest xmlns:android="http://schemas.android.com/apk/res/android" package="com.example.myapp">
<uses-permission android:name="android.permission.CAMERA" />
<uses-permission android:name="android.permission.INTERNET" />
```

```
<uses-permission
android:name="android.permission.WRITE_EXTERNAL_STORAGE" /> ... </manifest>
```

Furthermore, adopting secure coding practices is essential for preventing common security vulnerabilities, such as injection attacks, cross-site scripting (XSS), and insecure data storage. Developers should follow coding best practices, such as input validation, output encoding, and parameterized queries, to mitigate the risk of security flaws in their apps.

javaCopy code

```java
String username = userInput.getText().toString(); String password = passwordInput.getText().toString(); if (!TextUtils.isEmpty(username) && !TextUtils.isEmpty(password)) { // Perform authentication securely } else { // Display error message for empty input fields }
```

In summary, securing Android apps requires a multi-faceted approach that encompasses data encryption, permission management, and secure coding practices. By implementing robust security measures and adhering to best practices, developers can mitigate potential risks and vulnerabilities, safeguard user data, and build trust among users.

Performance optimization is crucial for ensuring that software applications deliver a smooth and responsive user experience across various platforms and devices. This chapter explores several techniques for optimizing the performance of software applications, focusing on memory management, network optimization, and UI optimization.

Effective memory management is essential for optimizing the performance of software applications, especially in resource-constrained environments such as mobile devices. Proper memory management helps reduce memory leaks, minimize memory fragmentation, and improve overall system stability and responsiveness.

One common technique for memory management is garbage collection, which automatically identifies and frees up memory that is no longer in use by the application. In Java-based applications, including Android apps, the garbage collector is responsible for reclaiming memory occupied by objects that are no longer reachable by the application.

javaCopy code

```
System.gc(); // Initiates garbage collection
```

However, relying solely on garbage collection may not always be sufficient for managing memory efficiently, especially in scenarios where memory-intensive operations are involved. Developers can optimize memory usage by implementing strategies such as object pooling, where reusable objects are maintained in a pool to minimize the overhead of object creation and destruction.

javaCopy code

```
ObjectPool<MyObject> objectPool = new ObjectPool<>(MyObject::new, 10); MyObject obj = objectPool.acquire(); // Perform operations with obj objectPool.release(obj);
```

Another aspect of performance optimization is network optimization, which involves minimizing network latency, reducing bandwidth consumption, and optimizing data transfer efficiency. One way to optimize network performance is through caching, where frequently accessed data is stored locally to reduce the need for repeated network requests.

In Android apps, developers can implement caching using mechanisms such as the HTTP cache provided by the OkHttpClient library, which allows responses to be cached based on cache-control headers sent by the server.

javaCopy code

```
OkHttpClient client = new OkHttpClient.Builder()
.cache(new Cache(context.getCacheDir(),
CACHE_SIZE)) .build();
```

Additionally, developers can optimize network performance by reducing the size of data transferred over the network, optimizing network requests, and leveraging techniques such as compression and minification to reduce the size of transmitted data.

UI optimization is another critical aspect of performance optimization, as the responsiveness and fluidity of the user interface directly impact the user experience. One common technique for UI optimization is layout optimization, which involves minimizing layout hierarchy depth, reducing view complexity, and optimizing view rendering performance.

In Android apps, developers can optimize UI performance by using tools such as the Android Layout Inspector to identify layout inefficiencies and optimize layout hierarchies for improved rendering performance.

bashCopy code

```
adb shell dumpsys gfxinfo <package-name>
framestats
```

Furthermore, developers can optimize UI performance by minimizing overdraw, which occurs when multiple views are drawn on top of each other, resulting in redundant drawing operations. Tools like the Android Developer Options feature "Show layout bounds" and "Show GPU overdraw" can help identify areas of overdraw in the UI.

bashCopy code

```
adb shell setprop debug.hwui.overdraw show
```

Moreover, optimizing resource usage, such as bitmap loading and image caching, can significantly improve UI performance by reducing memory consumption and rendering overhead. Techniques like lazy loading and bitmap caching can help optimize image loading and rendering performance in Android apps.

javaCopy code

```
Glide.with(context).load(imageUrl).into(imageView);
```

In summary, performance optimization techniques such as memory management, network optimization, and UI optimization play a crucial role in ensuring that software applications deliver a smooth, responsive, and efficient user experience. By implementing these techniques effectively, developers can improve the performance and efficiency of their applications, leading to higher user satisfaction and engagement.

Conclusion

In summary, the book bundle "Operating Systems 101: Novice to Expert" offers a comprehensive journey through various operating systems, providing readers with valuable insights and knowledge to navigate the intricate world of computing environments.

From the foundational understanding of operating systems with "Windows Mastery: A Beginner's Guide to Operating Systems" to the advanced techniques presented in "Unlocking UNIX: Advanced Techniques for Operating System Veterans," this bundle caters to readers at all levels of expertise.

"Linux Unleashed: From Novice to System Administrator" equips readers with the skills needed to become proficient in Linux, a widely used operating system in both personal and enterprise environments.

"IOS Demystified: Expert Insights into Apple's Operating System" offers an in-depth exploration of iOS, providing readers with expert-level knowledge of Apple's ecosystem and its unique features.

Lastly, "Android Engineering: Mastering the World's Most Popular Mobile OS" delves into the intricacies of the Android operating system, empowering readers to become proficient in developing and managing applications for the Android platform.

Overall, this book bundle serves as a comprehensive resource for individuals seeking to enhance their understanding of operating systems, from beginner to expert levels, across a diverse range of platforms including Windows, Linux, UNIX, iOS, and Android.

Whether readers are aspiring system administrators, seasoned veterans, or mobile app developers, "Operating Systems 101: Novice to Expert" provides the necessary tools and knowledge to excel in the world of operating systems.